D1246445

Young Man, You've Made My Day

A personal tribute to Brian Clough

MARCUS ALTON

Editor of brianclough.com

FOREWORD BY BARBARA CLOUGH

Proceeds to the Brian Clough Memorial Fund

BOOKCASE
EDITIONS LTD.

Bookcase Editions Ltd

Young Man, You've Made My Day
By Marcus Alton
Foreword by Barbara Clough

Published in 2008 by Bookcase Editions Ltd, 50 Main Street, Lowdham,
Nottingham NG14 7BE

ISBN 9780954782054

Jacket design and printing by Parker and Collinson Ltd,
42 Church Street, Lenton, Nottingham NG7 2FH

A catalogue record for this book is available from the British Library
ISBN 9780954782054

Young Man, You've Made My Day

Dedicated to Sarah - without whose unwavering love and support this book would not have been possible (and neither would the statue!)

Young Man, You've Made My Day

Young Man, You've Made My Day
Foreword by Barbara Clough:

When Marcus first approached me with the idea of this book I had no hesitation in giving it my full approval. I know it has been a labour of love for him - as have all the efforts to have a statue of Brian which now stands proudly in Nottingham city centre.

Marcus has created a wonderful tribute website. Brian was not really from the computer generation, but I am sure the website would have made him smile. He thought it was tremendous to receive all the messages from fans which were passed to him by Marcus - they gave him a real boost after his operation. Also, we as a family have very much appreciated all the e-mails and messages from fans that have been received by the website and forwarded to us. It is very comforting to know that Brian is still very much in so many hearts.

I think Brian would have been amazed by the success of the website, which has shown just how many fans he has all around the world. It is a fantastic tribute which I hope will continue for many, many years. I have often told Marcus that my eldest grandson is probably one of the website's biggest fans!

This book describes how the website was set-up and how it later became the official site of the statue fund. There is no doubt that the statue in Nottingham has been a magnificent achievement by everyone involved - not least by the small statue fund committee, comprising of a handful of volunteers who were brought together by Marcus. Their hard work and the generosity of all those who have supported the fund has been incredible.

When I first went to see the clay statue at Les Johnson's studio, it took my breath away. Les has done a remarkable job in capturing Brian exactly. I really like the pose with Brian's hands clasped together above his head, celebrating with the fans. Over the coming pages, Marcus describes the story behind the statue and how it all came together, as well as the times he met Brian and the campaign for a knighthood.

I hope you enjoy reading this book, which is a sincere tribute and an inspirational story of how a fan's dream really did come true.

Barbara Clough

Young Man, You've Made My Day

Contents

Young Man, You've Made My Day

With thanks to: Barbara Clough and her family, Doreen Elder and her family, Joe and June Clough, Paul Ellis, Mike Simpson, Rich Fisher, Mick Mellors, Paul Lowe, Les and Jennifer Johnson, Gary Lineker, John Motson, Jane Streeter, Ian Collinson, Colin Tarrant, Stephen Lowe, Alan Dossor, Cllr Jon Collins, Keri Usherwood, Stephen Barker, John Hewitt, all at Nottingham Forest, Sophie Stewart, Karl Cooper, Tim Wedgwood, Jon Douglas, John Lawson, Keith Daniell and The Media Group, Brian Tansley, Neil Hoyle, Doug and Joan Cooper, Will Sutton, Alex McKenzie, Andy Ball, the BBC, the Nottingham Evening Post; and not forgetting my Mum and Dad for their love and support and for encouraging my writing career from an early age!

Young Man, You've Made My Day

Chapter One
'Call Me Brian'

The moment when Brian Clough gave me a huge hug and kissed me on the cheek took me completely by surprise. I had heard he could be unpredictable. In interviews, some of his former players often recounted how it was best to expect the unexpected whenever the Master Manager was involved.

Even when his trophy-winning teams had returned to the dressing room after another fine performance, he would sometimes remind them in no uncertain terms that they should have played better. When they played poorly and lost (which was rare in the glory days), and the players feared the worst, he might tell them they had performed brilliantly and then put a consoling arm around the shoulder.

You never quite knew what Cloughie would do next. And that was the magic of the man. It was that magic which left me almost lost for words on the day he shared an unashamed display of emotion.

It was a Saturday morning and my mission was about to start. I decided to forego my weekend lie-in and instead went along to a village fete near my home, which was then on the outskirts of Derby. Although I was born in Nottingham, and grew-up in a Nottinghamshire village, I had moved along the A52 (now Brian Clough Way) for work reasons.

I read in the local newspaper that the special guest at the fete would be Cloughie himself. He had recently retired from football management but was still keen to help the local community by appearing at a fund-raising event. I went along not simply to catch a glimpse of my hero, but to ask him something. I hoped he would sign a photograph for me.

It wasn't just any old photo. This was a large and unusual picture of Cloughie in the dressing room with his victorious Nottingham Forest team after they had just secured their place in the 1991 FA Cup Final. It wasn't often that the Great Man invited the media into his dressing room, but on this occasion he had. The Reds had just beaten West Ham in the semi-final at Villa Park and the photographer captured a classic scene, with Cloughie sitting in his dressing gown alongside his players and backroom staff.

I had been in the crowd that sunny afternoon and celebrated as we looked forward to a trip to Wembley. The photo was a great memory of the day and I ordered the special black and white image from the Nottingham Evening Post. I was then determined to get everyone on the photo to sign it.

For several weeks I had waited outside the Forest dressing room after training sessions in the hope of getting the various players to add their names. And they all did. Roy Keane, rather shy in those days, carefully signed it for me, as did players such as Stuart Pearce, Des Walker, Brian Laws and Ian Woan. The backroom staff signed it too, as did Cloughie's son Nigel who is pictured with a towel round his waist. But the one signature which remained missing was that of Cloughie himself. So that Saturday morning, equipped with a black marker pen, I carefully took the photo with me in a large brown padded envelope.

It was a fairly low-key event and there was a small number of people waiting with me for Cloughie's autograph. The organisers had set-up a little table at which he proceeded to sign books and even scraps of paper. He took time to speak to everyone as we queued. Then came my turn. I carefully pulled the photo out of the envelope, wondering what his reaction would be when he saw it. His eyes lit-up as he gazed across that dressing room scene, as if the memories were flooding back. He could see all his players had signed it. "I wondered if you could sign this for me please, Mr Clough. Yours is the only signature I'm missing," I said, my hands trembling as I handed him the pen. "My pleasure, young man," came the reply, as he carefully started to add his signature.

Handing back the pen, he took one more look at the photo. "Happy days," he said, nodding. "Thanks Mr Clough, you've made my day," I said instinctively, my mouth dry with nerves. At that point, he looked up at me and got out of his chair. "Young man, you've made my day too," he said and stepped towards me. He opened his arms and gave me a huge bear hug and a peck on the cheek.

But a kiss was not his only gift when my girlfriend (now wife) Sarah and I met the Great Man some years later. He gave us a bottle of champagne. I am extremely fortunate that Sarah is almost as big a Cloughie fan as I am - she still treasures the photo she and her sister had taken with him when they were both Nottingham Forest Junior Reds. So when it was announced that he would be signing copies of his book 'Walking on Water' at a supermarket in Nottingham, we were both keen to meet our hero. It was August 17th, 2002 and the very first signing session he did for the book - in fact, the official publication date was several days later.

The publishers had confirmed he would be signing copies for the first 300 people who turned-up. Determined not to miss-out, we got there in plenty of time. In fact, we were the first to arrive - more than five hours before the Great Man was due to make his appearance.

Asda hadn't even opened its doors when we got there at about quarter to six in the morning. Not surprisingly we received some strange looks from some of the staff. They probably thought we were crackers. It was only when the doors opened at six-o-clock, and there were still no other fans around, that it started to dawn on us that we would be the first in the queue to meet Cloughie that morning. That thought made us feel even more nervous. What would he say to us? Would he tell us we were completely bonkers for waiting so long and send us away with a clip round the ear? Again, it was a case of expecting the unexpected.

As the queue behind us grew during the morning, the supermarket staff looked after us well and soon we were on first-name terms with them. They even made sure we had a drink and something to eat. Orange juice and doughnuts, I think it was. A table was set-out in front of us and copies of the new book were stacked-up in large piles, ready for the Master Manager to add his personal message. Eventually, the long line of fans snaked outside the main entrance. A huge sense of anticipation grew - after all, it's not everyday you see a footballing legend at your local supermarket.

Then, some five hours and fifteen minutes after we arrived, spontaneous applause broke out as Cloughie appeared from a side-door. The crowd sang his name, just like the Trent End used to during the Forest glory days, as he walked slowly towards the long queue inside the main entrance. For a moment he stood still with a big grin on his face and soaked-up the adulation. He blew a kiss and shouted above the singing, "Good morning to you!"

The outpouring of affection and respect from hundreds of people was quite overwhelming. And at the head of the queue, Sarah and I were both shaking with nerves as we prepared to meet the Legend. "Where's Sarah? I've been told I've got to meet Sarah," said Cloughie as he started to make his way through the crowd. An assistant from the publishing company realised it was going to be a difficult task for Mr Clough to get through the mass of people, so she guided him towards us. "Sarah's over here, at the front of the queue," she told him.

He walked towards us and, with a big smile, shook Sarah's hand and then mine. "It's great to meet you, Mr Clough," I said. "Nice to meet you too, young man," he replied, before asking where we lived. When Sarah said she came from Gedling, his eyes lit-up. "That's a pit area, isn't it? I've got a statue from Gedling Pit. They gave it to me." His support of the miners during the 1984 strike will live long in the memory of many people and it once again struck a chord with him on that sunny morning as he chatted to us.

Cloughie then presented us with a bottle of champagne for being the first in the queue. It was a bottle of Moet and Chandon - the significance of which was not lost on the Great Man himself. In the books he was signing that day, he admitted that drink had had an adverse affect on his health and there were times it had impaired his judgement. So, as he handed-over the champagne, he joked, "You're trying to get me on the booze again, aren't you?" The crowd laughed as they watched the Great Man, who was in fine form. A newspaper photographer, who knew Cloughie well, asked us to pose for a photo. Trevor Bartlett from the Nottingham Evening Post had worked with the Master Manager for many years and he captured some great pictures that day. As the three of us stood close together, Cloughie looked at me, smiled and joked to Trevor, "Hurry up, I've heard he's famous for getting people's wallets." There was more laughter.

Then Brian gave Sarah a kiss. It was a special moment and one I know Sarah will never forget. In fact, he kissed her on the cheek twice - to ensure Trevor got the photo. "Thank you, Mr Clough" she said, being careful not to drop the champagne. Cloughie pointed to the bubbly. "It goes well in the bath," he told us. "We used to bathe in that. It's easy when you win to have a glass of champagne. And the excuse when I lost was I thought I'd drown my bloomin' sorrows."

"But that didn't happen very often - you didn't lose many, Mr Clough," said Sarah, as Cloughie sat down to start signing our books. "That's right," he replied. "I had a good run, pet, I had a good run." And that must have been the understatement of the day. For Brian Clough to describe his all-conquering, trophy-winning seasons as 'a good run' was amazing. His achievements in turning an average second division club into European Champions and then re-building a squad to win the league cup and remain up there among the country's very best teams in the late Eighties was nothing short of remarkable. And the football was always entertaining and played in the right spirit. No answering back to referees. Unlike some of the top teams of the modern game. I am sure many managers these days would give anything for the 'good run' that Old Big 'Ead enjoyed.

As Cloughie began signing our books, I told him he was looking well. "Thank you - I'm feeling well," he said. "I've got five grandchildren, two of them boys - and they run me ragged." Despite the long queue behind us, Brian lavished his time on us. In an interview many years ago, he said he and his wife Barbara had brought their children up to be generous with their time and generous with their smiles. He was certainly abiding by that principle himself as we chatted to him. He said he couldn't believe we had bought about eight books for him to sign, many for our family.

Then came some advice. "If you get the chance, go and see a good side play - Burton Albion," he suggested. We were able to say we had already been to see the Brewers in action several times at Eton Park, where Brian's son Nigel became manager in 1998. Cloughie had a reserved seat there and we would always make a special effort to look-out for him. "It costs me a fortune at half-time for my grandchildren, with all the chips and burgers," he told us. "You'd think they never got fed at home!"

With everything signed for us, we started to pick-up our books and the champagne. We were still talking about Burton Albion. "Send Nigel our good luck," I said. "Yes, I'll pass it on," replied Cloughie. "It's been lovely to see you. Be careful going back - and thanks for coming to see me."

As the signing session continued, fans of all ages treasured their few moments meeting the Great Man. He took great care in signing each book - making sure names were spelt correctly and adding little speech marks above his famous message "Be Good." Many were meeting Cloughie for the first time. I watched as grown men, in awe of their hero, acted like shy schoolboys in front of the head teacher. One man said his hands had been shaking so much he could hardly sign his credit card slip. Showing their respect and admiration, the fans often addressed him as 'Mr Clough,' as I usually did. "Call me Brian," he once said to me. But it seemed strange being on first name terms with a football genius!

Another occasion I met Cloughie, and still called him Mr Clough, was at a dinner held in memory of the former England footballer Sir Stanley Matthews. It was May, 2001, and the event was at Stoke City's Britannia

Stadium. Cloughie was the guest of honour. The dinner was organised by the Sir Stanley Matthews Foundation, which was set-up in memory of the Stoke and Blackpool hero who won 54 caps for his country. The foundation was raising money for a statue and to help youngsters to get involved with sport.

As part of the dinner, the chairman of the foundation, Nigel Johnson, began a question and answer session with the Master Manager. But it soon became an enthralling speech, as the Great Man took the microphone, quite literally. "Your hand's shaking, I'll help you out, young man," he said as he took the mic from Nigel's grasp. There was instant applause from the audience. They then listened intently as Cloughie held court.

He paid tribute to the Wizard of Dribble. "Sir Stanley was not only a footballer, he was a magician," said Brian. "When it comes to great footballers, his photo is the one I show to my grandchildren. He was fantastic."

Among the topics he covered was his interview for the England manager's job. There was more spontaneous applause when he said the Football Association had made their biggest mistake when they failed to appoint him. "There were ten of them on the interview panel," he said. "And four of them had been dead for a year. What's more, the other six hadn't twigged.

"The FA feared that if I got the job, I would want to run the show from top to bottom. They were shrewd, because that's exactly what I would have done. We might even have won a pot or two!"

Some years later, readers of The Times newspaper voted Cloughie's absence from the England manager's job as one of Britain's biggest ever mistakes, alongside other errors such as Chamberlain's appeasement of Hitler in 1938. It is clear many fans still regret the fact Brian Clough was not given the top job.

Nevertheless, on that memorable night in Stoke, the Master Manager was the star of the show, honouring one of England's greatest players. He ended his speech with the words: "That's all for now. Go to bed." It was classic Clough.

Old Big 'Ead was then presented with a Sir Stanley Matthews Toby Jug, which was made locally. It was obvious he was genuinely touched by the surprise gift.

All this was a hard act to follow for the guest speaker for the evening, Derek Dougan. The former Wolves and Northern Ireland star said that of all the managers he had worked for, he would have liked to have played for Clough. Then a familiar voice added: "And if you had ever got your head to the ball, you wouldn't have so much hair!" Yes, it was Brian with another one-liner and Derek Dougan joined-in with the audience's laughter.

During the evening, a queue formed at Cloughie's table as people asked him to sign their pictures and menu's. He then helped to draw some of the winning raffle tickets. At the end of the night, it took him twenty minutes to leave the room as fans wanted to stop him and talk. He had time for them all - including me. I had taken my Dad, David, to the dinner and he managed to capture a magical moment for me on camera. I still treasure that photo of myself and Brian together at the end of that great night. It's the photo on the front cover of this book.

Looking back over the years, I realise I was very fortunate to meet the Great Man on a number occasions. Many people never get to meet their hero at all. Or when they do, sometimes the reality doesn't live-up to expectations. But that was never the case when I met Cloughie. Particularly one time when I least expected it. That was in connection with the tribute website....

Chapter Two
Cloughie Finds The Net

Brian's son Nigel was once asked by a local newspaper what he thought of the website I had set-up in honour of his father. "It's a nice tribute to Dad," he told the Middlesbrough Evening Gazette. That was shortly after I launched the non-profit making site in August, 2000. I was obviously delighted to read that - and I had to smile when Nigel added that his Dad wouldn't have known what a computer was if it bit him!

The Gazette, based in the town where Cloughie was born - and where he went on to set an amazing goalscoring record, devoted a large part of one its broadsheet pages to the report about the website, with an archive photo of the Great Man in action for Boro. The headline was spot-on: 'Cloughie finds the net - the world wide one this time.'

Shortly after that article, the Master Manager himself was asked on a radio phone-in what he thought to the website. "It's a good idea, son. Simple as that," came the reply. "If they've picked me for a website, why not?"

Cloughie's appreciation of the website and all the e-mail tributes sent by fans was clearly demonstrated some years later when he singled me out at one of his personal appearances.

He was signing books at a big store in Nottingham, just a few months after undergoing a liver transplant. The news of his life-saving operation in January, 2003, had taken many of his fans, and the media, by surprise. As a result, I had been inundated with e-mails from people wanting to send their good wishes and hoping that he made a speedy recovery. I was keen that Cloughie himself was able to read them.

The messages came from all over the country - and all over the world. Among the e-mails from overseas was one from a man who had been born in Cloughie's hometown and had since moved to Australia. Eric Carter sent the following message from Sydney: "Dear Brian, I wish you a speedy recovery from your operation. Like yourself, I was born in Middlesbrough and I started watching the Boro at the age of seven. I remember those goals you scored. In management you were a roaring success. An icon of the game. Thank you for many years of entertainment and enjoyment.

Get well soon."

There was also a very touching tribute from a fan in Canada. Bob Bradley had grown-up in Middlesbrough and followed Cloughie's career from the earliest days. He had lived in Toronto since 1963. "Brian," he wrote, "I have never written a 'fan' letter in my life and at 64 years of age I am very surprised that I would even bother at this stage of my life. However, I recently learned of your liver transplant and although you are recovering well, I just wanted to send you a note to wish you a speedy recovery. You brought much joy and excitement to me as a young soccer fan."

From the United States, Chris Brown e-mailed from Monroe in North Carolina. He wrote: "Mr Clough, get well. There is only one English gentleman who made such an impact on the beautiful game over the past forty years and we don't want to lose you just yet." Jim Corning in Columbus, Ohio, said he looked forward to many more years of Mr Clough's unique insight and opinions. "The volume of tributes from people all over the world clearly demonstrates the esteem in which you are held," he wrote.

Nottingham-born fan Neil Greaves sent a get well message from his home in Wellington, New Zealand. "Mr Clough, thank you for giving me the privilege of watching Nottingham Forest play such entertaining and winning football during your time as manager."

In another e-mail, there was a message you could perhaps imagine Clough himself giving to someone, if the roles were reversed. Keith Buttery wrote: "'Ere, Old Big 'Ead, get off that bed, it's not full time yet. Thanks for the memories."

Many fans wrote that they had been so pleased to meet Cloughie at his book-signings and were shocked to hear of his operation. Others wanted to simply thank him for the years of enjoyment he had given them. One man wrote from Saudi Arabia to say he was sure that fans all over the world were praying for the Master Manager. I was able to include the messages on the website, but was determined that Cloughie himself should see the admiration and good wishes that had been sent from around the globe.

Knowing it was highly unlikely that Cloughie would log-on to a computer to read the messages published on the website (even if a P.C. had bitten him by then!), I printed-off the e-mails and decided to take them to him in person. I was extremely apprehensive about delivering them to his house, but - given that he was not making any special personal appearances at that time - it seemed the best course of action to ensure he received them safely.

I knew Cloughie had moved to a house on the outskirts of Derby, not far from where I used to live. My heart felt as if it was in my mouth as I walked towards the front door, nervously clutching a large envelope containing a batch of e-mails wishing him a speedy recovery. I really didn't know what to expect. Would the Great Man himself answer the door? Would he give me a telling-off for disturbing him? After all, I was uninvited and he might think I was intruding on his privacy. But, on behalf of all the fans who had sent their goodwill messages, I felt I was doing the right thing. After a few moments, his wife Barbara answered the door. "Hello. I've brought these get well messages for Mr Clough," were the few words I managed to get out as my throat tightened with nerves. Mrs Clough smiled as I handed over the envelope. As I was about to turn to leave, she asked me where the messages were from. I explained they were e-mails sent to the website. Mrs Clough smiled again and thanked me, before I turned and headed for the main road, exhilarated that I had achieved what I set out to do. Some months later my instincts were rewarded when Cloughie remembered receiving those tributes - and the young man who had delivered them.

As I mentioned, he was signing books in Nottingham and a large crowd had gathered at WH Smiths in the Victoria Centre. It was a few months after the liver transplant and he was looking well. The queue of admirers eager to meet him began to spill out of the main entrance of the store. One fan arrived at six-thirty in the morning and waited for more than four hours to make sure he had a signed copy of the paperback edition of 'Walking on Water.' As Cloughie sat at a table signing books and other memorabilia, I was standing a few feet away, taking photo's for the website. His publishers were aware I was there and said I could stand two or three feet away from the queue in order to get the photo's I needed.

Suddenly, he stopped signing the books for the long queue of fans and looked-up in my direction. He pointed towards me and, slightly raising his voice, asked: "Are you the young man who brought that pile of messages for me?" I became frozen to the spot, like a rabbit caught in the headlights of a car. Was I about to get that rollicking I had feared for turning-up at his house unannounced? It was obvious he had recognised me, so honesty seemed the best policy. "Yes, Mr Clough, it was me," I replied. At which point he got out of his chair, leant forward and put his arm out to shake my hand. "Thanks very much for all those messages you delivered, young man," he said. "It was very much appreciated."

He then suggested we should have a chat, so at the end of the signing session we were taken down some steps to a room at the back of the store. Cloughie was accompanied by former members of his backroom staff at Forest, Ron Fenton and Archie Gemmill. The Great Man told me he was feeling well and it had obviously given him a boost to receive the messages of support. He was also impressed with the turn-out that day. "To see so many people has been nothing short of incredible," he told me. He spoke about how grateful he was to the NHS for his operation and that he hadn't received any preferential treatment in order to have the liver transplant. We also chatted about the fortunes of Nottingham Forest under Paul Hart, who was then managing them, and how his son Nigel's career had progressed since leaving the Reds. Those fifteen minutes in his company were like a dream come true. The photo's I took that day are still on the website, along with video footage. Again, it was an encounter I will never forget.

Looking back, it is hard to pin-point exactly when my admiration for Cloughie began. But it must have been around 1977, when I was taken to my first Nottingham Forest match. I was just nine years old and perched on the steps of the old East Stand. My Mum's friend Nora Armstrong took me to that first game - her family had been season ticket holders for many years. It was against Hull City in March, 1977, and we won 2-0. Forest were playing in the old Second Division and a certain Garry Birtles made his debut. Not that I remember much about the game itself. But the sheer atmosphere in the ground was enough to get me hooked and I saw several more games that season. In those days, I was allowed to clamber over the turnstile for two or three matches, without paying admittance, and the turnstile operator received a bottle of whisky at Christmas. It would never happen now of course - and neither would they allow rival fans in front of us to throw darts at each other. "Put your hood up and you'll be OK," I was told as the little weapons flew from one side to the other.

As Forest's meteoric rise up the football ladder began, I was swept along too. I watched transfixed as this charismatic figure called Brian Clough led the previously little-known Nottingham Forest to European glory. Still just a young lad, I would record his interviews off the radio or television and onto my little mono cassette recorder. Carefully timing the questions and his answers, I would record over the interviewer's comments to make it sound as if I was interviewing the Great Man himself. Little did I appreciate that in years to come I would have the opportunity of interviewing him face to face.

In later years I had a season ticket in the Trent End before moving to the Upper Tier of the Executive Stand, which has since been renamed after Cloughie. That was built on the site of the East Stand, on the opposite side to the dug-out. There, I had a grandstand view of the Great Man in action. Shouting instructions, pointing, directing his team and ultimately soaking-up the adulation of the fans. Even before the matches kicked-off, I would eagerly look-out for that figure in the green sweatshirt emerging from the tunnel, taking his seat in the dug-out and acknowledging the chants from the crowd as they sang his name. "Brian Clough's a football genius," was a favourite chant in the Trent End. And it became the title of my tribute website.

Back in the year 2000, I was astounded there was no dedicated website in honour of my football hero. Despite having no knowledge about how websites are created, I decided to have a go. The idea began during a conversation with a friend and colleague, Tim Wedgwood. He explained to me how it was possible to buy domain names - ie the names of websites. First you had to establish that no-one else had bought the name. Within a few mouse clicks we had confirmed that the name 'brianclough.com' was available. I couldn't believe it. Not only was the name available, but it was a dot-com - the best option, I was told. Suddenly the dream of setting-up a website in tribute to Cloughie started to become a reality.

I had no experience at all of what was required to start a website, so I spent hours learning the technical aspects from a book. A lot of it was trial and error. In fact, the word 'error' seemed to appear on my computer screen quite frequently! Just when I thought I had mastered another step in the process, that unwelcome word would return to haunt me. Having planned the basic editorial content of the site, all I wanted to do was publish it. But the days spent tackling the technical problems soon became weeks. Eventually I cracked it. The index page, or home page, was published and the website was gradually built. At that point, few people knew about it and that suited me fine. I needed time to build more content and ensure that my aptly-named email address 'youngman@ brianclough.com' was working. I also made sure I wrote to Mr Clough to let him know of my intention to launch the non profit making website and to say I hoped he liked it. Once everything was in place, I chose a launch date, August 8th 2000, and sent out press releases to publicise it. The start of the football season seemed a good time to kick things off - and I wasn't disappointed. The website attracted coverage in the local and national media. The launch was even mentioned twice in the same edition of The Sun newspaper - once in the news section and again in the sports pages. I was interviewed for newspapers, radio stations and for television.

As the publicity grew, I was soon receiving e-mails from Cloughie fans across the UK and around the world. Among them was a tribute written by Joe Appleby from the wonderful address of Lookout Mountain, Georgia, United States. He explained that during his childhood he lived on the next street to Cloughie in Middlesbrough. "We played against each other in competing street teams on Clairville Common. It was Valley Road v Eden Road. I also remember that in our family you couldn't say a bad word against Brian Clough." He explained that his late mother was a cleaner at Brian's school and she had nothing but praise for the Head Boy of Marton Grove. "I left England in 1963 for Canada and USA but I kept-up on Cloughie's career. He certainly added a little Boro spice to the game, and the game is all the better for it."

From Washington DC, David Lovato wrote: "Wow! What a treat to find a Brian Clough tribute site, and one that appears worthy of his extraordinary accomplishments in every sense!" The former Nottingham student had lived next to the City Ground and started watching Forest when they were in the Second Division. "Brian Clough was at the centre of this storming assault on the established 'great powers' of football," he said.

The website also inspired a Derby County fan in Johannesburg, South Africa, to get in touch. Mike Trapido was full of praise for Old Big 'Ead. "The man had class. He was not only a great tactician but a wonderful man-manager long before the term became fashionable. His use of the carrot and stick has never been bettered. They all believe you need money. All Cloughie ever needed was Cloughie."

The international appeal of the website has been clear not only through the tributes and messages of support, but the fantastic response to the competitions it has featured. Prizes have ranged from signed books and sweatshirts to T-shirts and DVD's. Among the more unusual prizes were two green sweatshirts made in tribute to the Great Man and signed by his sister Doreen when I visited her in Middlesbrough (more about that later!). There was an overwhelming number of entries for that competition and one of the winners, picked at random, came from Singapore. The other winner was from Nottingham. In May, 2004, the prizes were Cloughie T-shirts. One of the winners had e-mailed from the Greek capital, Athens. Pavlos Argyriadis had studied in Nottingham and promised to wear the special piece of clothing in tribute to the Master Manager during the Olympic Games in Athens later that year.

The prize in the website's first competition was a bronze coin in a presentation box, marking Cloughie's achievements with Nottingham Forest. There was such a large response that the sculptor who had donated the prize, Gordon Brown, agreed to offer a second coin. One of the winners was Frank Swain in Alberta, Canada, while the other was Mick Tucker from Cramlington in Northumberland. They were both later linked-up on a live radio programme and interviewed by BBC Radio Nottingham. Frank, who was originally from Nottingham, said he emigrated in 1977. "It was very bad timing," he admitted. "It was a shame to miss-out on the glory years with Brian Clough, but it was nice to see the club get some success." Mick was born just two miles from Cloughie's birthplace. He was presented with his prize at a special event at Gordon Brown's craft centre in Nottinghamshire in March, 2001, and has kept in touch with me ever since. He told me: "That was a fantastic day and the coin is something I will always treasure."

The success of that first competition was reported on the website's news pages, which have reflected a variety of stories over the years - a few of them sad, some serious, many up-lifting and others which are more light-hearted. I was once contacted by a Nottinghamshire woman who was compiling a charity cook book and wanted to get in touch with Cloughie. The result included the Master Manager's menu for his favourite three-course meal. The tasty treat began with smoked salmon followed by saddle of lamb and finished-off with home-made rice pudding.

And long before that, there was the news of Operation Clough, launched by Police in Staffordshire. It emerged that Old Big 'Ead's no-nonsense footballing philosophy had inspired a crime-busting initiative. There were a number of arrests and the recovery of thousands of pounds worth of drugs. Apparently, the operation reflected Cloughie's simple approach to management. A clear case of 'Clough on Crime, Clough on the Causes of Crime.'

On the subject of the Police, I was contacted by a Sergeant from the Nottinghamshire force who had a special memory of the Great Man.

Brendon Hunt spotted himself in the photo of Cloughie being mobbed by fans, which is on the front page of the website. The picture was taken at the end of Brian's last league game at the City Ground, when Brendon was on duty. He is the policeman pictured just behind Cloughie's right shoulder. "Funnily enough, I wasn't a football fan at the time and that day I had no idea that it was Brian's last match," said Brendon. "It didn't dawn on me, until I saw the footage many times on telly, on the internet and in the papers, what a really momentous day it was." He remembers the fans surging onto the pitch to surround their hero. And somehow he found himself on the grass with them.

"I recall pushing through the crowd, who were making towards Brian, and with two or three other officers formed a Police cordon around him, to offer him some protection from the crowd who were simply mobbing him. He looked tired and almost beaten, and perhaps a little overwhelmed. I said to him, 'Are you alright Brian?' and he replied, 'Oh yes, young man!' and he continued to conduct his pitch farewell. I don't really remember how Brian escaped the pitch invasion around him, or really what happened next, but this pitch walk seemed a long and exhausting one."

Of course, it was a very emotional day - Cloughie's final home league match, against Sheffield United, which saw the Reds relegated. Even the United fans sang his name and Cloughie acknowledged them with his famous thumbs-up. Ever since that day, Brendon has been a Forest fan. "I try to get to the City Ground as often as I can, and the events of that day come back to me each time I go. I mainly sit in the Brian Clough Stand and try to recall which set of stairs I was standing on when the pitch was invaded, but I can't. I can just remember whereabouts I was on the pitch when I came face to face with Brian Clough, and an event I shall never forget."

While that photo of Cloughie surrounded by fans will always be special for Brendon, another picture on the website means a great deal to me personally. I would never say I was anything like a professional photographer, but I have to admit it is one of the best I've ever taken. And it was from some distance too! The Master Manager was visiting the City Ground to watch his two former teams, Forest and Derby, battle it out in the East Midlands derby in September 2003. He arrived forty minutes before kick-off and initially waited in the reception area of the club he once ruled from top to bottom. I was standing in the Main Stand car park, some thirty feet away from the Great Man, and managed to take the photo - and several others. It helped that the door to the reception area was slightly open, allowing me a clear view even though I wasn't very close. I love the photo because it wasn't posed and captures Cloughie in a relaxed mood, perhaps sharing a joke with someone. I'm even more proud to say that his sister, Doreen, has a copy of it framed on her wall at home.

A few months before I took that photo, Cloughie had made his first public appearance since the liver transplant. It was at Burton Albion's Eton Park ground as he watched Nigel's Albion side beat Chester City two-nil. One fan, Ruth James, later e-mailed to tell him: "Great to see you at the Burton Albion match. You certainly brought us good luck, Brian, with this fantastic win. Hope you continue to make good progress." The following month, I saw Cloughie at Burton's home match against Stevenage Borough. He was on top form and signed autographs while sitting in the stand. He told me he was feeling well. That day, I was lucky enough to take the first public photo's of him following the operation.

It was obvious that his fans were overjoyed at seeing him in public again. I even received an e-mail from a fan in the United States later that year, when the Master Manager returned to his old club Middlesbrough to watch them play Arsenal. The Sky television cameras had shown him in the stand before the game, in August 2003. Watching in Charlotte, North Carolina, Tony Hodgson wrote: "Saw you on telly at the game...you look great. No player or manager had more heart than you."

There was also a big cheer at Forest's City Ground when Cloughie sent a special message to supporters during the match against Wolves in April that same year. As the two sides started the second half, the electronic scoreboard displayed the words: "To all my friends and fans at Nottingham Forest. Thank you for the cards and beautiful flowers while I've been off colour. From Brian xx."

The year 2003 was the tenth anniversary of the Great Man's retirement and, to mark it, my website launched a special poll. Fans were invited to vote for the top three players who served Cloughie during his managerial career. The names of all fans who entered were put in a prize draw to win a copy of his autobiography, 'Walking on Water,' signed by the Great Man himself. The poll saw the former Scottish international John Robertson voted Brian's best ever player. The top three included Stuart Pearce and Archie Gemmill, while other names put forward by supporters included Roy Keane, Peter Shilton, Kenny Burns and John McGovern.

The signed book went to Richard Dennys from Bristol. Richard replied: "Thanks so much for the book. I am especially pleased with a signed copy. For years I had kept a personal letter written and signed by Brian Clough, enclosing four free tickets to Forest v West Ham for my grandmother, which is the reason I have supported Forest ever since. The letter was lost in a move years ago, so the signed book goes some way to replacing it."

But that vote for Cloughie's all-time best player was not the only poll which the website has run. I also asked fans to vote for his best ever quote. And with all the fantastic one-liners the Master Manager gave over the years, there was a tremendous response. That list of classic Clough comments will always make fantastic reading.

Chapter Three
In The Top One

There is no doubt that when Cloughie spoke, people listened. The football commentator, John Motson, once described Brian Clough as the most compelling interviewee he had ever met. In fact, when he was preparing to interview the Master Manager for the first time, Motty says his editor told him that Old Big 'Ead could even have read the telephone directory and it would still have made gripping listening. Cloughie could be a journalist's dream. Once a reporter was fortunate enough to secure an interview, it would be an odds-on certainty the Great Man would produce a headline-grabbing quote. In some cases, the words from just one interview would land like gold-dust which could then be sprinkled out over several articles.

Cloughie was king of the one-liners. In fact, the actor Colin Tarrant (who portrayed him brilliantly in the tribute play 'The Spirit of the Man') told me that he thought Clough could have had a fantastic career as a stand-up comedian, if he hadn't been so successful as a football manager. Indeed, a poll by a digital TV channel in 2007 named the Master Manager in the top ten of Britain's greatest wits of all time. The survey put him at number nine, in the company of Shakespeare and Noel Coward (Oscar Wilde was top of the list).

So there is little surprise that one of the most popular pages on my tribute website features many of Clough's classic quotes from over the years. I spent hours compiling the list - trawling through magazine columns and countless interviews in newspapers and on television and radio. Up until the website, there was no single comprehensive list of his greatest comments. In fact many of the quotes I collected, particularly from television and radio interviews, were not documented for posterity until the 'Classic Quotes' page appeared. One newspaper had attempted to list some of his great comments in 1999, but unfortunately they were not as memorable as the ones on the website - as was shown following the Great Man's sad death in 2004, when the national media used the website as an instant reference point for those brilliant one-liners. Many of the national newspapers printed the list straight from the 'Classic Quotes' page and I felt immensely proud that my work (a labour of love!) was used in this way.

The quote I am most proud of capturing for posterity came in a television interview in 2001, although it received little, if any, national coverage at the time. It was an interview conducted by a regional television station. Cloughie was talking about his Forest 'Dreamteam' - the best players who served him during his 18-year reign at the City Ground. Reflecting on his success, he commented in typical style: "I wouldn't say I was the best manager in the business, but I was in the top one." Yes, it was a quote that summed-up Cloughie's public persona brilliantly and I was determined it should be written down and documented forever. In 2004, many of the obituaries in the media featured that comment prominently and I am sure it once again prompted a few knowing smiles from his fans during what was a very sad time.

That quote was voted the fans' all-time favourite in the website's on-line poll, the Quote Vote. The results were released in the week the Great Man celebrated his 67th birthday in 2002.

In another interview about that 'Dreamteam' he spoke about how difficult it was to choose his best ever Forest side. Naming Garry Birtles and Trevor Francis as his two strikers, he added: "It's that good a team my son can't get in it - and he's the second highest scorer in the history of the club. I think he's entitled to ask if there is a place for him on the bench!" And yes, Nigel was named among the five substitutes. Cloughie said later: "He got more stick from me than any other player but came bouncing back and always did his job to the best of his ability."

During his retirement, Cloughie enjoyed many hours watching Nigel's Burton Albion side. After one match he produced another humorous one-liner, even though it was at his son's expense. Interviewed after Burton beat Farnborough two-nil, he told the Brewers' match-day programme that it made his week when Burton did well, especially when they kept a clean sheet. He joked: "I was actually hoping that Burton would lose today because I was going to put in for the job if they sacked the manager."

In reality, Cloughie was hugely proud that his son was starting on the managerial ladder at Burton. When the Brewers prepared to play an FA Cup tie against Old Big 'Ead's former club Hartlepool in 2003, he had a choice phrase to show that he did not interfere with Nigel's job and that his son was his 'own man.' In the days leading up to the televised match, father and son posed with the FA Cup at a local school. Clough Senior was asked whether Burton would win and whether he had any tips for Nigel. He responded: "Anyone can win in the FA Cup. That's the magic of it.

The good, the bad and the ugly can beat the rich, the famous and the talented. And the only tip I give Nigel is, 'get off the M1 when it's foggy.' "

In another interview, Brian insisted he kept his opinions to himself when he watched Burton. And there followed another great quote: "The only comment I've made is to the chairman, to tell him his meat pies are awful and that I could recommend a better supplier."

When it comes to demonstrating that Cloughie himself was most certainly his 'own man,' there is one particular comment which stands out. It came in a television interview, in the early days of his managerial career. Filmed in black and white, a young-looking Clough was asked how he responded to a player who disagreed with him. He replied: "We talk about it for twenty minutes and then we decide I was right." Priceless.

That philosophy on dealing with certain players could also be extended to football chairmen and directors, who were often at the sharp end of his comments. Referring to those directors who he described as knowing nothing about football, he once said: "The only match they've seen is in a box of Swan Vestas." And he was angry about chairmen who sacked managers on a regular basis. In one interview he described them as "a pack of wolves devouring everything in sight." Cloughie said he wanted to see a new regulation introduced to make such chairmen accountable for their actions. "There should be a rule that if the manager goes within a year, then the chairman goes with him."

Cloughie's simple philosophy about how the beautiful game should be played also led to one of his most enduring quotes. Stressing the importance of passing to feet, without ugly long balls booted high from defence to attack, he commented: "If God had wanted us to play football in the clouds, he'd have put grass up there."

It was that type of entertaining and incisive comment which led a radio station to invite Old Big 'Ead to be their match summariser for Derby County's home game against Manchester United in March 2002. The Master Manager was full of praise for United's Ruud van Nistelroy, who collided with the Rams keeper Andy Oakes in the opening minutes. Cloughie described the striker as being brave. "He didn't look for the goalkeeper, he got his head to the ball. Is he a Dutchman? Considering the Germans got through Holland in ten hours, he was brave for a Dutchman." During the same match, the Master Manager also made a cheeky comment about a male streaker who ran onto the pitch. "The Derby players have seen more of his balls than the one they're meant to be playing with," he joked.

The team from Old Trafford was certainly on the receiving end during a BBC interview in which he was asked for his opinion on United opting-out of playing in the FA Cup one year, so they could play in the World Club Championship. "Manchester United in Brazil?" Cloughie asked in amazement. "I hope they all get bloody diarrhoea." On another occasion, at a football forum in 2002, United's manager, Sir Alex Ferguson, was the subject of another Cloughie wisecrack. Referring to the two consecutive European Cups that the Master Manager had won, he commented: "For all his horses, knighthoods and championships, he hasn't got two of what I've got. And I don't mean balls!" Cloughie said later it gave him a feeling of satisfaction that Sir Alex had not won two successive European Cups or led a team to 42 unbeaten league games, particularly with the type of scant resources Old Big 'Ead faced. But it's also worth pointing out that in an interview in 1999 he said Sir Alex had done a fantastic job as United manager.

On the subject of Manchester United, Cloughie was often complementary about David Beckham when he played for Sir Alex - although he wasn't a fan of some of his hairstyles! Neither was he an admirer of Victoria Beckham's singing. And in 2001 he was amazed to hear about the content of Posh Spice's missing luggage during a trip to America. "Who the hell wants fourteen pairs of shoes when you go on holiday? I haven't had fourteen pairs in my life." That one makes me laugh every time I read it.

Fans often ask whether Cloughie could have managed the young, multi-millionaire celebrities of today. I reckon he could have done so very effectively. When he was asked in a newspaper interview how he would approach that type of challenge he replied: "A bit of fear, a bit of the father, a bit of friendship. If a player comes into a manager's office he shouldn't sit down unless he's invited to do so. No matter who he is. The father figure should be strict but fair and deserve the respect."

During his retirement, Cloughie was often asked about the influx of players from abroad. In his first ever radio phone-in, he commented: "I can't even spell spaghetti never mind talk Italian. How could I tell an Italian to get the ball? He might grab mine." On another occasion, he was asked about Derby County's Fabrizio Ravanelli. "The nearest I've got to Ravanelli is in the Co-op. They sell it in tins."

And in an interview in The Times newspaper in 2003, he expressed his concern about the amount of foreign influence on the British game. Asked whether he liked going abroad, he replied, "No...I don't really see the point of it. Too many foreigners."

But the great quotes didn't end there. He also had a way with words when talking about the fans' campaign to secure him a knighthood.

Chapter Four
A Knight To Remember

When Cloughie was asked in a radio programme whether he knew who had nominated him for a knighthood, his response was as sharp as the sword which should have been gently placed on his shoulders by the Queen. "I thought it was my next door neighbour, because I think she felt that if I got something like that, I'd have to move."

Although the Great Man gave a light-hearted response, he also spoke quite modestly about the nomination - which may seem quite surprising, given how outspoken he could be on other issues. "I knew nothing about it at all...I've got a couple of achievements along the line somewhere. You get to know nothing about these things until they are actually on your doorstep."

The knighthood campaign started shortly after my tribute website was launched. I was soon receiving e-mails from Cloughie fans - and one of the common themes was the injustice they felt that the Master Manager had not been made a 'Sir.' Yes, he had been awarded an OBE (which Cloughie said stood for Old Big 'Ead!), but many people wrote to say he deserved the ultimate honour.

One of the first e-mails, back in August 2000, came from Paul Greenfield in Southend. He described himself as neither a supporter of Forest nor Derby but "always a Brian Clough fan." He praised Cloughie's managerial skills and the way his teams played. "His achievement of taking Forest to a European Cup within two years of being in the Second Division will never be equalled," he said. Urging the start of some kind of campaign for a knighthood, he added: "If Alex Ferguson gets knighted for winning the European Cup once with the biggest side in the world, then Brian must be knighted - he won it twice with a smaller club. Arise Sir Brian Clough."

The strong feelings among those who emailed me quickly became overwhelming. But I knew that if a campaign was to attract the national attention required, it needed the backing of some famous names. Among the first of the big names to give their support was the 'Match of the Day' host and former England striker Gary Lineker. Within days of writing to him I received a letter, personally signed by Gary, offering his support. On

9th October, 2000, he wrote: "I wish you every success with your campaign to get a knighthood for Brian. He was indeed a great manager and also quite a character."

And talking of former England strikers, there was also support from Trevor Francis - the man who scored the winning goal in Forest's first European Cup Final. I wrote to him at Birmingham City, where he was the manager. Again, there was a prompt reply. In a letter written on the club's headed paper, he asked me to add his name to the campaign and wished me good luck with the venture. I also contacted another European Cup winner from Forest's glory days, who was then assistant manager at Middlesbrough. Viv Anderson replied: "I am delighted to support you in your endeavours to secure an honour for Brian - he has been a great servant to the game and richly deserves this recognition."

My next letter went to the very top. It was dated 21st October, 2000, and was addressed to the Prime Minister, Tony Blair, at Ten Downing Street. The letter explained the strength of feeling expressed in e-mails to the website and named Gary Lineker, Trevor Francis and Viv Anderson as high-profile figures from the world of football who were keen to see Cloughie knighted. I enclosed copies of their letters and asked for Brian Clough's name to be considered when the Honours List was drawn-up, either in the New Year or for the Queen's Birthday in 2001.

At this stage, I was eager for the campaign to attract the attention of the media. With big names already giving their support, I sent out a press release announcing that fans had now started a campaign to honour Cloughie with a knighthood. The release - dated Tuesday 24th October, 2000 - named Lineker, Francis and Anderson as backing the calls for a 'K' and explained that a letter had been sent to the Prime Minister. I felt this was a crucial first step in raising the profile of a campaign which had been inspired by the fans, while hoping that those with the power to make decisions would treat the matter seriously.

The subsequent publicity generated by the press release, including coverage in newspapers and on radio stations, prompted a deluge of further e-mails from fans offering their support. One Nottinghamshire woman got in touch to say she was writing on behalf of her 72-year-old mother who was not computer literate but, from the publicity, had taken the trouble to write down the website address and asked her daughter to put forward her vote. Her message was: "Knight Mr Clough, he deserves it a lot more than some of the bu****s that receive them." The daughter added: "Excuse her French, but at 72 she expresses her views quite strongly these days. Please also add my vote, my husband's and daughter's. Brian Clough deserves a knighthood."

Within days, the website was receiving e-mails from fans of many different football clubs - all wishing the campaign well. Queens Park Rangers supporter Peter Leavy described Clough as a magnet for affection throughout the football world. "In my mind I knighted Brian years ago, that it is not official is almost criminal," he said. Another fan offered his 'wholehearted' support and stated that Clough represented everything that was great about the game. "He is to football what Einstein was to physics," he said, before describing Clough as "a genius who is long overdue recognition of the highest order." Luton Town supporter Gavin Sharp said there was no question that a knighthood was deserved. "His knowledge and grasp of the game would teach many so called managers of today a lesson or two."

The feelings of many people were summed-up in an e-mail from Steve Farmer who considered himself to be very fortunate to have supported Forest during Cloughie's reign. He wrote: "Brian Clough gave hope to every football fan in the country that one day their club could make an impact." Derby fan Stephen Baker added: "If the knighting of Alex Ferguson sets the precedent, then Mr Clough OBE should be given two knighthoods." That message reminds me of a comment which was said to be one of Cloughie's own favourites: "That was such a blatant penalty, it was two penalties!"

Another fan went even further, suggesting the Great Man should become a Saint. Mark Cartledge wrote: "His contribution to our domestic game was so mammoth that he should have received a knighthood years ago. I whole-heartedly support the campaign for this long over-due award (personally I think the man should be cannonised)."

A fellow Clough admirer believed the campaign for a 'K' should be plain sailing - he had named a boat 'Sir Brian.' Simon Constance wrote to say he'd been a Forest fan for thirty years and had officially logged the name of his boat on the small ships register. "I have always felt that Cloughie should have been knighted," wrote Simon. "I often get asked about the name and it gives me great pleasure to explain what Cloughie achieved with the resources at his disposal, when compared with other 'sir' managers that football has recognised. To this day, not one person has disagreed that Cloughie should be knighted, although the vast majority are supporters of teams that Cloughie did more harm to than good." Simon sent a photo of the boat, which I featured on the website.

As the e-mails continued to stack-up, I decided to send a follow-up letter to the Prime Minister and enclosed as many of the messages of support as I could. Within a few days came a reply. Dated November 3rd, 2000, the letter was sent by David Spooner in the Nominations Unit/Ceremonial Branch of the Cabinet Office. He said the Prime Minister had asked him to thank me for the two letters and the enclosed correspondence. The closing sentence was the most important: "I shall ensure that your recommendation receives most careful consideration." At last, it seemed those in power were aware of the growing calls for the ultimate honour.

Through the power of the internet, the knighthood campaign soon took-on a life of its own. Having received a promising reply from the Cabinet Office, I drafted another press release and that led to further publicity. By then, the website had received more than 300 e-mails of support, including many from all over the world, as well as the backing of a leading MP. I had written to Joe Ashton, who was the chairman of the all-party football committee at the House of Commons. He replied: "I will be happy to nominate Brian Clough but I have to tell you that in the past 30 years I have made 30 nominations and not one was chosen. The great and the good at the top of the Football Association have a big say in these things, but he may be lucky."

As the publicity grew, former Clough players added their support after being asked in interviews what they thought of the knighthood campaign. Garry Birtles, who scored his first Forest goal in the European Cup tie against Liverpool, told a commercial radio station: "There's no doubt he deserves a knighthood for what he achieved." Former Forest captain John McGovern said a knighthood would be a fitting tribute. He told an interviewer: "Any honour that is given to Brian Clough is fully deserved due to his fantastic record in football. A unique man with a unique record. There is no other manager to touch him."

It was still crucial to keep the campaign in the public eye and thankfully a press release, dated Friday December 8th, 2000, had the desired effect. There were soon articles in the local and national press, as well as reports on the radio and television. On that day alone, the website received the largest number of hits it had ever had in twenty-four hours (nearly 700), along with more than 100 e-mails (although that record has since been broken). There is no doubt that response was the direct result of the fantastic coverage in the media. I could not have hoped for anything better.

'Arise Sir Clough' was the headline in the sports pages of the Daily Mirror. Its football writer David Moore produced a glowing report about the Cloughie knighthood campaign and 'the efforts of his worldwide legion of fans.' He said the Master Manager was an obvious candidate for a knighthood - although he admitted it would be interesting to see what would happen once Cloughie met Her Majesty again. "One can imagine the Buckingham Palace banter right now: 'Hey, young lady, just watch what you are doing with that sword.'"

Throughout the efforts to try to secure a 'K' for Cloughie, I was very impressed by the coverage from all sections of the media. Later in the campaign, a regional newspaper had the front page headline: 'A Knight to Remember.' In December, 2000, a national tabloid splashed the headline, 'Arise Sir Big Head!' alongside a big picture of him holding the European Cup.

Then came a very public endorsement from Cloughie's former England colleague Jimmy Greaves. In his weekly column in The Sun newspaper, 'Greavsie' said the Great Man deserved a lot more than an OBE. He said a knighthood would be a fitting tribute for what Cloughie had achieved at smaller clubs and he didn't understand why the Master Manager had been ignored. He said there were few men more worthy of the honour in the recent history of football. The support of such a well-known and well-loved figure as Jimmy Greaves gave the campaign a huge publicity boost.

Greavsie's opinions were shared by a fan who e-mailed me from Toronto in Canada, following the coverage of the campaign on the internet. Neil Cresswell had been a season ticket holder in the City Ground's Trent End before emigrating. "I sincerely hope he is knighted and soon," he wrote. "It seems the people in power have made a point of ignoring Brian throughout his career, ignoring him or fearing him." From Singapore, Rupert Keeley offered his support too. "His ability to produce great teams from minimal resources is unrivalled. I'd love to see him honoured in this way."

Closer to home, Paul Walker from Derby commented: "If he had been manager of a big name club or a London club he would not have been overlooked for so long."

Andy Scott in Newark, Nottinghamshire, summed-up the feelings of many when he wrote: "If people are to receive recognition for services to the community, Brian Clough should receive a knighthood for all his work for the City of Nottingham and many charities, as well as what he did for the footballing communities of Derby and Nottingham Forest."

Indeed, Cloughie's charitable work and generosity, which often went unreported, was another major factor in his knighthood nomination. Even back in 1980 he was quoted as saying he received hundreds of letters every week, many of them requests for good causes. "I feel there is a moral and social obligation on us to try and help those in need," he said, adding that he had a lot of interests in charities but he regarded them as very personal. I was once told by a very reliable source that Cloughie had received a request to visit a terminally-ill youngster in hospital. The visit went ahead, and no doubt meant a lot to the child and their family, but it was all kept top secret at the time. Cloughie wanted to avoid any media coverage about it. He did not want to appear to be seeking publicity from what was a personal and private visit. I am sure that is just one of countless stories that could be told.

The Great Man's generosity was also demonstrated through an e-mail I received from a former Nottingham nurse who had since moved to the United States. Tina Chetwynd-McHargue e-mailed from Oregon with memories of watching the Master Manager's Forest teams and his help for a fund-raising appeal. Her e-mail read: "Mr Clough, you once donated a Forest plate to the Nottingham City Hospital Renal Unit. I was raising money to take the transplant patients to the British transplant games. What a roll it started. We had so many gifts donated after we received yours. We raised more money than any other year. And what a time we had at the games. Thank you for your generosity, thank you for the memories. We love you."

The impact that Cloughie had on so many lives could never be underestimated. Just a few minutes that people might spend in his company often meant a memory that would last a lifetime. For some, even a few seconds was enough. I received an e-mail from a man whose late father was an admirer of the Master Manager and was keen to see him during an open-top bus tour following another Forest Wembley trip. Ian Macbriar and his Dad had been standing on Trent Bridge to watch the bus go past. "My Dad was looking for the Great Man, who was sitting at the back of the top deck. As the bus came alongside, Dad shouted up 'Brian.'

The Great Man stood up and looked down over the side of the bus. They made eye contact and exchanged thumbs-up signs. I honestly thought my Dad would have passed away in that moment. The knighthood is long overdue."

Another fan e-mailed to say that his family had been guests at a Forest match and were able to introduce a disabled friend to Cloughie. "He spent time with our friend and hugged him. He spontaneously arranged for the Forest goalie to take him out to take penalties at the Trent End. All this just an hour before his team were due to play. This memory will never leave our friend or his family. Please knight him and give him the status he deserves."

On a personal note, I remember waiting outside Derby's Pride Park Stadium with my Dad to see Cloughie arrive at an awards ceremony in April, 2001. It was raining and we and the other fans who had gathered at the main entrance were getting absolutely soaked. The Great Man arrived with his wife Barbara and walked up a red carpet and into the building. Seeing the fans getting wet outside, he insisted they be allowed into the foyer and he signed books and photographs, including a book for my Dad. That night, Old Big 'Ead received a Lifetime Achievement Award, presented by the then Derby County manager, Jim Smith. It was part of an event organised by a radio station.

Just a couple of months earlier, Jim Smith had also backed the knighthood campaign. In a personally-signed letter on Derby County headed paper, he wrote: "I add my support in your venture to get Brian Clough knighted. He truly deserves this prestigious award for everything he has achieved in the world of soccer."

Back in the world of Westminster, I had also received support from the Nottinghamshire MP and Forest fan, Kenneth Clarke. The former Chancellor had told me he thought the knighthood nomination was a good idea and he would do his best to help. However, he suspected that the "peculiar system that organises these things" would mean the fact Cloughie already had an OBE could count against him.

Nevertheless, Mr Clarke pursued the matter and within a few weeks he forwarded me a letter from the then Secretary of State for Culture, Media and Sport, Chris Smith. Mr Clarke had taken-up with him the suggestion of an honour for Cloughie. The letter from Mr Smith was dated December 12th, 2000, and referred to my correspondence with the

Nottinghamshire MP. In reply, Chris Smith wrote to Mr Clarke: "Nominations and letters of support are extremely valuable to the honours process so I am very grateful that you have written. I will ensure that Brian Clough's case is given full and careful consideration at the appropriate time. You will understand, however, that I am unable to offer you any guarantee as to the outcome." In Kenneth Clarke's accompanying letter to me, he added: "These things are treated with strict confidentiality, and we will now have to await developments."

When Cloughie's name was left out of the 2001 New Year Honours List, there was understandably a lot of disappointment among fans. "It is unbelievable that Brian Clough has once again been neglected," wrote Tony Glover in an e-mail. "Let us hope that the powers that be come to their senses the next time."

Despite the set-back, it was vital not to lose the campaign's momentum. It was time for another press release - and the letters I'd received from Westminster were just the ammunition I needed. 'Campaign Receives Vital Boost' was the title of the release dated January 5th, 2001. It explained that fresh impetus had been added following the intervention of Kenneth Clarke and that the Culture Secretary would ensure the nomination was considered carefully. "The letter from Chris Smith gives us fresh hope for success," stated the release. As a result, there was more coverage in the media to highlight the efforts behind the scenes.

The continued publicity, including reports on various football club websites, meant the campaign even reached Japan. In February, 2001, Nick Doan sent an e-mail from Tokyo, where he was working. He said the ultimate honour would be fully justified. "Surely, it's no more than he deserves," he wrote. "The man is an ambassador for the sport and it's time he was acknowledged." Support was also offered by the Australian and New Zealand branch of the official Forest Supporters Club (Nottingham Forest Supporters Down Under). The chairman and founder of the branch, Todd Street, wrote: "There could be no more suitable an honour for a man so loved by so many people." Further on-line backing was given by the Sunderland Independent Fanzine, 'Ready To Go.' They set-up a special e-mail link so fans could add their messages to the campaign. One of the many resulting e-mails came from Bryan Forster. "If Alex Ferguson can be knighted for winning one European Cup with a club the size of Man Utd, then why not Brian for winning two with a 'small town' team like Forest? Continued injustice in my opinion."

The campaign was also a talking-point at a Legends Evening at Forest's City Ground, hosted by my friend Brian Tansley. Former Reds favourite and England player Steve Hodge was applauded as he paid a glowing tribute to Clough. "The words genius and great are used far too often in football," said Hodge. "There are few great, great managers, but he was one of the best and he should definitely be a Sir."

To ensure the spotlight was kept on the campaign, I wrote to the Cabinet Office again in March, 2001, reminding them of what had been said before and how disappointed fans had been after the news of the previous honours list. If decisions were being taken behind-closed-doors, in the run-up to the Queen's birthday in June, I reckoned that a timely nudge could make all the difference along those corridors of power.

Within a few days of sending the letter, a reply landed on the doormat. It was from another case officer in the Nominations Unit, who thanked me for my correspondence. Dated March 12th, 2001, the letter read: "I can well understand your disappointment that Mr Clough has not yet received a further award. The competition for Honours is highly competitive and it is inevitable that the number of nominations we receive far exceeds the number of awards available and, at times, good candidates do not succeed against stronger competition. I can confirm, however, that Mr Clough's claims continue to be considered fully and carefully." I was extremely pleased to receive that personal reply from an official in the Cabinet Office (who had signed it personally too) and the final sentence still meant there was hope for the future. But could there be such a thing as stronger competition? The e-mails I had received demonstrated loud and clear that fans thought otherwise.

Determined to keep up the pressure, I sent a timely letter to the Culture Secretary, Chris Smith, reminding him of Cloughie's nomination. On Mr Smith's behalf, a reply was sent by the Honours Secretary in the Public Appointments and Honours Unit. Diane Macfarlane's letter, dated April 4th, 2001, again thanked me for getting in touch. "Please be assured that Mr Clough's contribution has not been overlooked," she said. "He remains under consideration for future honours rounds, but for reasons you will understand there can be no guarantee as to the eventual outcome."

Another press release, sent out towards the end of April, maintained the campaign's momentum. It referred to the correspondence from government officials as well as the additional backing of Derby County's

Jim Smith. "Fans of the Great Man are not giving up hope," was one of the sentences in that release.

But there was further disappointment when Cloughie's name was left out of the Queen's Birthday Honours List for 2001. While motor racing's Jackie Stewart improved on his OBE with a knighthood, there was no place for the Master Manager. So the efforts to get our man on poll position for the next list were stepped-up a gear.

A Cabinet reshuffle meant Tessa Jowell had succeeded Chris Smith - and it was time to make her aware of the fans' feelings. Another letter was posted, accompanied by many of the e-mails of support. This time the letter began by asking the new Culture Secretary whether she could 'succeed where your predecessors have failed.' The reply, some weeks later, came once again from Diane Macfarlane, the Honours Secretary. Thanking me for the nomination, she apologised for the delayed reply. The letter continued: "I can assure you that Mr Clough's case remains under consideration for future honours rounds. I should add, however, that we receive many hundreds of nominations for honours every year and there is fierce competition for the limited number of awards available. I cannot therefore give any indication of when Mr Clough may be included in one of the honours lists."

While that letter offered some hope, another letter I received that November gave the campaign a further boost. It came from Paul Hart, the then manager of Nottingham Forest and a former Cloughie player. Indeed, Harty was determined to re-introduce many of the Clough values to the club, both on and off the field. His letter to me offered his full support for the knighthood campaign and he wished me good luck with my endeavours. That kind of backing fuelled further publicity, which in turn generated more e-mails. I received an e-mail from the sports editor of an English language newspaper in Tenerife. John Riddle wrote: "I remember seeing Cloughie play for Sunderland and Middlesbrough. When he came to Hartlepool United, the club I have supported since 1957, the whole town was buzzing. When we were promoted with the team Cloughie built and John McGovern, a Hartlepool lad, went on to lift the European Cup twice, the people of Hartlepool were proud. Arise Sir Brian!"

Unfortunately, those last few words were not forthcoming following the publication of the 2002 New Year Honours List. Despite the Great Man's name being missed yet again, fans continued to declare their support. Mark Raven, a Burton Albion fan, e-mailed in January 2002, describing Cloughie as the greatest football manager that ever lived. "I have met the Great Man twice and, despite his nickname of 'Old Big 'Ead,' I found him charming, humble and approachable," wrote Mark. "He did not know me from Adam, yet he took the time to speak to me and listened to what I had to say." The e-mail concluded: "His service to the country and his place in the heart of millions of people cannot be ignored. Give the man a knighthood. Sir Brian Clough would be a fitting and appropriate title for such a great man who has brought so much pleasure to so many people."

Over the next two years, the website continued to receive e-mails in support of the campaign, from fans all over the world - from Manchester to Malaysia. Barry Johnston wrote from Westfield in Western Australia: "It is a disgrace that Brian Clough has not been knighted. England made the tragic mistake of not making him their manager when they had the chance. A knighthood would go some way to rectifying that error."

Yet, still there was no sign of the ultimate honour being granted. But just when it seemed all possible avenues had been explored, and that even the support of famous names had drawn a blank, the campaign took on a new lease of life. Suddenly there was a fresh impetus. It was a kick-start which saw thousands of fans respond at football grounds up and down the country - and inspired more big names to give their backing. It led to a memorable trip to Downing Street and coverage by the world's media. Yes, just one telephone call changed the whole direction of the knighthood campaign.

Chapter Five
The Road To Downing Street

The telephone call came out of the blue. But it helped to dramatically change the whole dimension of the campaign to get Cloughie a knighthood. The man who made the call was the then chairman of the Nottingham Forest Supporters Club. Mel Hart told me he'd been forwarded a letter by Forest, which I might be interested in. The letter had come from a Reds supporter and Cloughie fan who was keen to see if a petition could be started. Mel asked me whether I'd be interested in speaking to the author of the letter, Mike Simpson. It proved to be the catalyst for a new chapter in the campaign.

Mike Simpson's admiration for Cloughie is beyond question - although the thought of his first 'close encounter' with the Great Man still makes him wince today. Mike and a friend had been standing around the back of the City Ground's Main Stand at half-time during a match and noticed that the dressing room window was open. They edged closer and tried to eavesdrop on what was being said. A few moments later that famous head popped through the window and told them in no uncertain terms to make themselves scarce - otherwise they'd be thrown out of the ground. Understandably, they did as they were told. Years later, Mike's second 'close encounter' was a lot more friendly. It was at a book signing - just as memorable but not so dramatic.

Mel Hart arranged for me to meet Mike at a hotel just off the A52 between Nottingham and Derby (now Brian Clough Way). During our chat, Mike explained that it was back in the Fifties when he first saw the Great Man in action for Middlesbrough against Forest at the City Ground. Decades later, he was hailing a football genius. His letter to Nottingham Forest described it as a 'travesty' that the Master Manager had not received the same honour as other football legends such as Geoff Hurst, Tom Finney, Bobby Charlton and Bobby Robson.

As we talked for more than an hour it became clear to me that here was another fan who felt as passionately as I did - and was fully prepared to do something about it. Mike had already written to two local MP's, Geoff Hoon and Liz Blackman, who had each sent him an official nomination form for national honours. But he felt that wasn't enough. Taking the website campaign a step further, he planted the seed of an idea: a petition in which fans would be asked to sign forms in support of the knighthood proposal.

"If we could get some petition forms made and get supporters to sign them, it might make all the difference," he said. "I'd be prepared to go down to the City Ground and collect signatures on a match day. You never know, it could work."

I told Mike that I liked the idea. But I pointed out that a big petition would probably involve a lot more work than one or two individuals could manage on their own. To work effectively, it would need the assistance of supporters groups up and down the country. Thankfully, the Nottingham Forest Supporters Club offered help with the proposal. In April 2004, Mike and I met Paul Ellis and Mick Mellors from the supporters club, again at the hotel on the A52. Paul had succeeded Mel Hart as the supporters club chairman and said he was willing to see what could be done to help with a petition at the City Ground. Mick was also very enthusiastic and volunteered to collect signatures. They also supplied a list of supporters club branches so that petition forms could be e-mailed directly.

I contacted supporters groups at other football clubs and received an encouraging response. Sarah helped to design a petition form which was then e-mailed to those who wanted to get involved. But I felt the campaign needed a focus - or event - to help it succeed and capture the imagination of the fans and media alike.

Looking at the football fixtures, I could see that many of Cloughie's former clubs were playing at home at some point over that August Bank Holiday weekend. It seemed an ideal time to ask fans to sign petition forms at the various football grounds - and generate maximum publicity across the country. Many of the supporters groups I contacted were enthusiastic and keen to be involved, so petition forms were either posted to them or e-mailed.

At that stage I had absolutely no idea how many signatures we might get. But as the plans began to take shape, I was eager to make sure that - whatever the number of signatures - all the forms and e-mails would find their way to the very top: Ten Downing Street. With that in mind, I contacted the MP Bob Laxton, whom I had originally met when he was a city councillor in Derby many years earlier. Bob had since become the MP

A favourite photo. Brian Clough photographed by Marcus during a visit to the City Ground in September 2003.

Above: Champagne Moment. Cloughie presents Sarah and Marcus with a bottle of bubbly after they waited over five hours to see him at a book signing. Photo courtesy Nottingham Evening Post.

Below: Pitch-side Presentation. Receiving petition forms from volunteers at Nottingham Forest's City Ground. With Marcus are (from left) Supporters Club chairman Paul Ellis, Mick Mellors and Mike Simpson.

Above: Boro Backing. Marcus (fourth from left) collects the knighthood petition from supporters at Middlesbrough's Riverside Stadium. "I'll never forget just how friendly the fans were."

Below: Happy Memories. Sarah and Marcus meet Cloughie's brother Joe and sister Doreen in Middlesbrough to hand over a copy of the knighthood petition.

Above: Taking it to the top. Marcus with MP Bob Laxton outside Number Ten, Downing Street, with the knighthood petition. This photo was taken by Sarah who helped to make the presentation.

Below: Next stop - £60,000. Actor Colin Tarrant joins statue fund committee members alongside the Brian Clough tram at the fund's official launch in June, 2005.

Above: The Banner Men. Statue fund chairman Paul Ellis and actor Colin Tarrant are filmed with two of the banners donated by Nottingham City Council from the civic tribute and later auctioned for the fund.

Above: Wogan's Winner. Marcus makes a special presentation to Mrs Clough during a Gala Dinner for the statue fund. It was a signed tribute from Sir Terry Wogan, one of Cloughie's favourite radio presenters.

Left: On The Ball. Former Nottingham Forest star Martin O'Neill signs a designer football donated to the fund by Sir Paul Smith.

Above: Picture Perfect. Actor Colin Tarrant is joined on stage by Nottingham Forest legends alongside a photo which they signed - it was then auctioned off for the statue fund.

Above: That Green Sweatshirt. Cloughie's former secretary Carole Washington is pictured with statue fund chairman, Paul Ellis, as she buys one of the fund's tribute sweatshirts.

for Derby North and was in fact Cloughie's MP. I wrote to him at the House of Commons asking if he would help present the final petition forms at Number Ten later that year. Due to security measures, I knew that special appointments were needed to gain access to Downing Street and therefore the involvement of the local MP would be invaluable. Thankfully, Bob remembered me and replied that not only would he support the knighthood campaign, but he'd be pleased to also help present the petition.

In order to allow enough time for all the petition forms to be collected after the Bank Holiday (including those sent by post), I suggested at that stage that the presentation should be late September or early October. Bob pointed-out that due to the party political conference season, the House of Commons was not sitting between mid-September and mid-October. So we provisionally looked at late October for the grand presentation to be made.

'Sign up for Cloughie' became the slogan over the Bank Holiday weekend, as another press release hit all the right buttons as far as the media was concerned. I had already secured the backing of two more leading managers and their comments were included in the release. At Charlton, Alan Curbishley added his tribute to Cloughie, saying "he'll always be a Sir in my eyes." He described Brian's managerial career as "second to none, a feat that will never be equalled again." The Sunderland boss Mick McCarthy also supported the campaign, adding that Cloughie would be a "worthy recipient" of a knighthood.

During the week leading up to the big petition I was interviewed on radio stations and television. National and local newspapers also gave the campaign lots of positive publicity. The more interviews I did, the more optimistic I became. The press release had explained that there was added urgency because a committee of MP's had concluded that the honours system was too secretive and suggested that knighthoods should be phased-out altogether. It was a race against time. "This is one last push to get the ultimate honour for Brian Clough," declared the release.

As the media coverage continued, the campaign received a major boost when the manager of Cloughie's former club, Middlesbrough, gave his emphatic support. Steve McClaren's comments were reported first on the club's official website. He described Cloughie as a legend of the game and said his goalscoring record at Boro had demonstrated he was something special. "But there is no doubt that his managerial achievements, especially with Derby and Nottingham Forest, make him a very obvious candidate for a knighthood," he said. I printed-off that page of the club's website and included it in the petition which was later handed to the government.

To make it easier for me to collect the petition forms from individual fans, I decided to set-up a PO Box number so they could return them in the post. Every couple of days or so, I would visit the local Royal Mail Sorting Office in the hope that more forms had been completed. I felt a huge sense of anticipation each time I walked up to the counter and explained I had come to collect mail for Box 8213. That was often followed by an even greater feeling of satisfaction when I was handed a pile of thick envelopes containing the forms. I think it cost me about £43.00 to have the PO Box number for six months, but it was well worth it.

Then the 'Big Weekend' arrived. That sense of nervous expectation returned. It was time to see just how strongly grassroots supporters felt about the knighthood campaign. Would they take the time to stop on their way into the football grounds and sign a petition? Volunteers were geared-up to collect signatures at a number of grounds, including outside Forest's City Ground, Middlesbrough's Riverside Stadium, Pride Park Stadium at Derby and Sunderland's Stadium of Light. I had also contacted fans groups at Hartlepool United and Burton Albion, with both clubs playing at home on Bank Holiday Monday. The very thought of galvanising the support of fans around the country in a direct 'call to action' sent a tingle down the spine.

At the City Ground, I was part of a small group of volunteers collecting signatures ahead of the Reds' game against Coventry City. I decided to stand near the entrance to the Main Stand car park, while several others were positioned on the other side of the ground, near the Trent End. The response of the fans was superb. As I stood there with the petition forms, supporters actually queued-up to add their names. Well-known faces also gave their support. The former Forest star Kenny Burns stopped to sign a form on his way into the ground. Even the Coventry manager Peter Reid signed-up shortly after stepping-off the team bus. That was all due to the quick-thinking of Mike Simpson, who seems to know no fear when it comes to standing-up for Cloughie - he managed to elude one of the security staff in order to secure Reid's signature. As the number of signatures grew, the television cameras arrived and I was interviewed about how well all the efforts were going.

I'm pleased to say hundreds of fans signed the petition outside the City

Ground in the two hours before kick-off. Given the small number of volunteers (and the limited amount of time to catch people on their way into the stadium) it was a fantastic achievement. The Supporters Club collected further signatures for the campaign and, two weeks later, presented me with forms containing more than seventeen-hundred names. It was a proud moment as I stood at the side of the City Ground pitch for the match-day presentation of the forms at the game against Cardiff on September 11th, 2004.

In addition to the outstanding efforts in Nottingham, I was absolutely overwhelmed by the reaction in Middlesbrough. I had been in touch with Boro's Official Supporters Club and its then chairman, Stuart Bargewell, was extremely keen to be involved. He was confident there would be a very positive response. They circulated the petition before the match against Crystal Palace and collected more than two-thousand signatures in just ninety minutes before kick-off. It was an incredible contribution and a week later Sarah and I went up to the Riverside Stadium to meet the volunteers. They presented me with all the forms and it was an absolute privilege to meet people who felt as passionately us - people like Sue Gardner who I know worked flat-out to ensure it was a success.

The kindness and friendliness of the supporters in Middlesbrough that day is something we will never forget. Stuart and his wife Sue organised an impromptu tour of the stadium for us, even though it was a Sunday. They introduced us to one of the officials there who had fond memories of Cloughie. Stuart explained to him that we were visiting after organising the knighthood campaign. His eyes lit-up and we were treated like royalty as he took us behind the scenes of the stadium, including the changing rooms. Stuart and Sue then asked if we would like to see some of the Cloughie landmarks in the town. How could we refuse? Over the next couple of hours we were taken to see the house on Valley Road where Cloughie was born; nearby Albert Park, where he spent many carefree hours; the church where he and Barbara were married; and the site of Rea's Café (which had since become a modern restaurant), where Brian met Barbara and where he often discussed footballing issues with his then Boro team-mate and later managerial partner, Peter Taylor. The photo's I took of those special places are on my tribute website - on a page entitled 'The Land of the Legend.'

A week after the trip to Middlesbrough, I drove to Derby County's Pride Park Stadium. I had arranged to meet a Derby fan who had performed a stirling job in collecting signatures before the Rams' home match against Crewe. Marcus Shukla had contacted me offering help with the petition. He told me how he had once been Cloughie's paperboy and received some practical advice from the Great Man. Out on his paper-round one day, Marcus had become absolutely soaked during a downpour. Cloughie saw him and told him to get home quickly and dry-off before he caught a cold. It was advice not to be ignored! So, there we were, many years later. The two Marcus' - one from Nottingham, the other from Derby - standing outside Pride Park, united in honour of our hero. The Ram handed petition forms to the Red. Overall, Marcus, along with other Derby supporters groups, collected more than six-hundred signatures. I also received e-mail support from the then Labour leader of Derby City Council, Chris Williamson, and his fellow councillor Richard Gerrard.

A little further down the A38, I went to see the editor of the fanzine at Burton Albion. Karl Savill, the man behind the aptly named 'Clough the Magic Dragon,' had done a great job in collecting signatures. In fact, the first name he secured was that of the club chairman, Ben Robinson. On the day Karl presented me with the completed petition forms, I remember sitting in the stand at Eton Park while the announcer on the public address system reminded people at the match to add their support. He explained it was a campaign by the website, brianclough.com. It made me smile to then hear a lady sitting behind us comment with surprise to her friend, "Ooh, he's got his own website - that's very good, isn't it?" When Cloughie himself arrived at half-time and took his seat in the stand, the collection of signatures was conducted carefully and in hushed tones - even the announcer was careful not to give the game away!

Alongside all the work of the volunteers at the various football grounds, the website was still a focus for fans' support. Over a ten-day period either side of that Bank Holiday weekend, the site received nearly two-thousand hits. Many of those visits resulted in fans sending individual e-mails for inclusion in the petition bundle. I even received signatures from Thailand, which were faxed to me by an ex-pat out there. A Nottingham sports bar also agreed to have petition forms - the Southbank Bar collected over seven-hundred names. There was great coverage of the campaign in the various football club match-day programmes and on their club websites - I've no doubt it helped to inspire fans to sign-up.

Even though many supporters could not be there in person to add their names, the strength of feeling came through very clearly in the e-mails. Just a few days before the big petition weekend, Jim Wood e-mailed from thousands of miles away to offer his backing for a knighthood for Cloughie. He wrote: "I well remember seeing him at Ayresome Park when I was a boy, and have followed his career from then to now. Alas, I am in Australia and unable to attend any functions in England, but I will be there in mind. All the best with your quest and may a very successful and colourful player/person be repaid for his services."

From Bridgetown, Barbados, Ian Rollitt e-mailed his support: "The greatest football manager of all times. He should have received recognition 25 years ago. Now is the time to correct the injustice." Closer to home, Sam Neal e-mailed from Stapleford in Nottinghamshire: "Brian is a true national hero and gentleman who deserves this long awaited accolade to comfort him in his twilight years."

I continued to receive e-mails of support into September. One notable message came from Derby season ticket holder Sue Allen, who had a special reason for giving her backing to the campaign. She met Cloughie when her Dad was terminally ill. Her father was 'Mac' - the Rams bootman from 1946 until his untimely death in 1973. She wrote: "Brian was so kind to my Mum during a very difficult time and came to my Dad's funeral, slipping in quietly, sitting unobtrusively at the back of the Crematorium and leaving very quietly too, so as not to take any attention away from the main event. This was a side of him not often recognised by those who only think of him as Old Big 'Ead. A great personality and manager."

On the day I received that e-mail, I sent a letter to the Manchester United manager, Sir Alex Ferguson. I thought that if he would add his name to the cause, it would give the campaign a vital extra boost. Sir Alex was kind enough to send a reply, personally signed. But he said he could not support the campaign. In a letter dated September 13th, 2004, he wrote: "Unfortunately I never really got to know Brian, although we were contemporaries and great rivals, and I feel that only those people who really know the man personally should be supporting this campaign. I am sorry that I cannot be of more help."

I told Mike Simpson about the letter and he shook his head in disbelief. "That letter was very disappointing," he told me later. "Other football managers and leading figures from the sport were only too willing to support the campaign, even though I doubt they knew Cloughie personally. They admired what he had achieved and knew he deserved the honour. So I was baffled by that letter. Cloughie himself had previously stated Sir Alex was deserving of the title. It was just a shame the complement could not have been returned." Years later, Sir Alex kindly opened the new stadium at Nigel Clough's Burton Albion.

Despite the response from Sir Alex, I received a very positive letter from the commentator John Motson. On 'Match of the Day' headed paper, he wrote to say I could add his name to the campaign. "I believe he deserves the honour because no other manager has won the English Championship with two such unfashionable clubs and also two European Cups. Good luck!" Having won the backing of another high-profile figure such as 'Motty,' I felt confident there would still be plenty of potential publicity in the run-up to the presentation of the petition in Downing Street. That was still planned for late October, after the MP's had returned from their party conferences. By mid-September it seemed most of the hard work for the campaign had been completed successfully. Thousands of people had given their support. With that in mind, Sarah and I decided to take a break for a few days in France. But within hours of arriving there, we received some devastating news.

Chapter Six
Goodnight Young Man

Nothing could have prepared me for the telephone call I received on September 20th, 2004. Sarah and I had just arrived at an hotel in Disneyland Paris at the start of a four-night break, away from it all. We were sitting in the bar area having a drink when my mobile phone rang. I was surprised I hadn't switched the phone off as it was the beginning of our holiday. But, in hindsight, I think I was meant to answer that call. It was a colleague of mine in Nottingham, Diana Peasey, and what she told me left me stunned. She said Brian Clough had passed away that morning in hospital and the news was about to be broadcast on the radio. Knowing that I am such a huge Cloughie fan, and ran the tribute website, she wanted to ensure that I was one of the first to be told the devastating news.

For a few moments I sat there, the phone pressed against my ear, as I tried to comprehend what Di was telling me. She explained that a statement from the hospital said Mr Clough had died from stomach cancer. Listening to my side of the conversation, Sarah could tell it was bad news. I thanked Di for calling me and, for a few minutes, I sat with Sarah as the news began to sink in. I felt numb, as if a member of my own family had died. Cloughie had been looking so well when I had last seen him. The liver transplant had given him a new lease of life. So this news was a huge shock to me. Suddenly, sitting in the hotel in Disneyland seemed completely the wrong place to be. Both Sarah and I felt terrible and it was made much worse by being hundreds of miles away from home.

My thoughts turned to the thousands of fans who would want to pay tribute to the Great Man and express their thanks for the years of enjoyment he brought them. My website would be a focal point for them and I knew I had to find a computer quickly. But getting access to the internet was easier said than done. Sarah and I went to the hotel reception and explained the circumstances: I needed urgent access to a computer with internet access, so I could update my website - and I was willing to pay whatever it may cost. But there were blank faces on the other side of the reception desk. Not because of any language difficulty - they could understand what I was asking for. But the staff could not give me access to a computer - all the internet connections for guests were wireless, so you had to have your own laptop in order to log-on to the worldwide web. To say I felt frustrated was a massive understatement. How many families take a laptop with them on holiday? At that point, as I stood in the hotel lobby, my mobile phone rang again and it was the first of many calls from the media asking for interviews.

The next few hours were a mixture of emotions - devastation at the loss of my hero, accompanied by sheer desperation as we tried in vain to find access to the internet. And I tried to keep it all under control as I did one radio interview after another on the mobile phone in Disneyland. Eventually, the hotel staff suggested a well-known restaurant might be able to help with the internet connection. It was a short walk away, but again turned out to be fruitless. Both the restaurant's computer terminals, which offered pay-as-you-go internet access, were out of order. I just couldn't believe it. However, one person I thought might be able to help was hundreds of miles away in Nottinghamshire. That was my friend and colleague Karl Cooper, who knew how to log-in to the website controls in order to edit it. Karl had previously given me some invaluable advice on how to update the site even when I wasn't at home (provided there was access to a computer!). He had also set-up a message board for fans to leave their tributes, which operated in addition to the e-mail option.

But to add to the frustration, Karl's phone was switched off and I had to leave a message. And still the phone rang with interview requests from radio stations and newspapers. Fortunately, Karl called back within a couple of hours and I was able to dictate over the phone the exact changes I wanted to make to the website content, to reflect the sad news. He also helped to change the way visitors could access the message board, making it easier for fans to post their tributes on-line instantly. Instead of new visitors having to register to use the message board, and waiting for me to approve their membership, their tributes were published straight away.

The following morning, I spoke to Karl again when he interviewed me on the BBC Radio Nottingham Breakfast Show. Speaking as a fan, and the editor of the website, I did the interview on my mobile phone, sitting in the hotel bedroom. Although I didn't know what questions Karl would ask, I had a reasonable idea - especially after all the interviews I had given the day before. Nevertheless, the final question hit me very hard and I wasn't expecting it at all. Karl led-up to the question by saying that with a bereavement, people often don't get the chance to say goodbye. He asked me to imagine that Brian was looking down on us at that moment - and what would I say to him?

Full of emotion, I replied by saying that, through the knighthood campaign, Cloughie would have already seen the genuine affection thousands of fans felt for him. Then, as my voice began to falter a little, I added: "If he was looking down now, I'd say 'Thanks Brian for all the great times. You were a great manager and we'll miss you very much.'" At that point I had to pause and explained it was a very emotional moment for me. Knowing I was on live radio, I composed myself as best I could and added, "You were a one-off, you'll never be replaced, we'll always be thinking of you and we'll miss you." Even now, listening back to that recording, I still feel very emotional. But I think the interview summed-up how I felt at the time - and still do.

Later that morning, with all the interviews concluded, Sarah and I made our way to a cyber-café several miles from the hotel. A tourist information service had suggested it as a good place for reliable internet access. The journey involved a short trip on a train and we found it without too much of a problem. I paid up-front for use of the internet and I spent a few hours there that morning, updating the website and responding to e-mails, while Sarah waited patiently. We made several visits to that internet café over the next few days. I can't tell you how grateful I was we found it - and how much I appreciated Sarah's understanding and patience.

As we walked past a newsagents at a train station in Paris, I noticed that many newspapers featured Cloughie on their front pages. I heard a young French girl say his name as she pointed to one of the tabloids. Several papers had a certain quote - my favourite - alongside their headlines: "I wouldn't say I was the best manager in the business, but I was in the top one." Back home, my family and friends saved me copies of the national and local newspapers. 'Goodnight Young Man' was the front page headline in the Nottingham Evening Post, accompanied by a photo of Cloughie holding the European Cup.

One of the common questions I was asked in the various media interviews I gave was whether the knighthood campaign would continue. To me, there was no doubt about the answer. The campaign would carry on and the petition would be handed in at Downing Street. Bob Laxton told me he was still willing to help present the petition at Number Ten in October. I felt the job was not yet done and we owed it to the thousands of fans to see it through to the end.

Sarah and I flew back home in time to join the thousands of people at the Civic Tribute in Nottingham's Old Market Square. We watched the archive footage on the large screen and listened to Cloughie's captain, John McGovern, as he paid tribute from the balcony of the Council House. He told the crowd: "If ever I need memories of Brian, I just have to look at my medal cabinet - it's full of them."

From there, we made our way to the City Ground, where Forest held their own tribute before the match against West Ham. We stood in silence, looking at all the flowers and scarves which had been left by fans. And in amongst them we found the floral tribute I had ordered via my Dad while we were in Paris. It was accompanied by a message I had written on behalf of all the fans who visited the website. Sarah took her own personal tribute and laid it carefully with the others. Along with some flowers, she had printed out a special message next to the photo of her with Cloughie when she was a Junior Red.

Inside the ground, we applauded as the many trophies won by the Great Man were displayed in the middle of the pitch, before some of his former players walked around the centre circle. I was so pleased Sarah was with me to see that. Fortunately, while we were in Paris, I'd asked my Dad to go to the City Ground and buy a ticket for Sarah so she could sit next to me in the Trent End. Much of the game was played in brilliant sunshine. And that warm glow around the ground became even stronger when Forest won with virtually the last kick of the match. Perhaps someone 'upstairs' had the final say on the matter: "It only takes a second to score a goal."

After the match, it seemed a long walk back to the car, as we reflected on all that had happened - not only that day but during the previous week. But the emotional rollercoaster had not finished its journey just yet. As I reached the car, a colleague was waiting for me. It was Neil Heath, a fellow Forest fan and a talented artist. From a large, thick envelope, he produced a framed picture of Cloughie which he had painted. "I thought you'd like this, it's for you," he said, handing me the gift. I looked at the picture - that famous green sweatshirt, the familiar face. And the tears I had been holding back all day finally appeared. I gave Neil a big hug and thanked him for such a wonderful thought. It may sound strange, but I felt I had been through so much over the previous few days, that this gift went a little way towards helping to cope with it all.

The sadness I felt was shared by the hundreds of fans who e-mailed the website or left tributes on the message board. The site received thousands of hits, or visits, over just a few days. On September 20th alone, there were 14,000 hits. But the increased activity meant the site - which I had set-up purely as a hobby - exceeded its usage allowance for the month and I was sent a bill for over £500 by the company which provided the webspace. However, when I explained the circumstances they reduced the bill by half. The e-mails I received from fans came from as far afield as Cambodia, New Zealand, the United States and Australia. One of the messages was from the daughter of Cloughie's football boss when he was in the RAF. She had arranged for the two men to be re-united in the 1980's. "It is a sad loss. Brian was unique," she wrote. Mick Applegarth e-mailed from Middlesbrough and described Cloughie as the best centre forward he had the privilege to see. He added: "As a manager he was simply the best. I met him at a school athletics meeting when I was a kid. He shook my hand when he presented me with a medal and I did not wash my hand again for over a week."

Fans of many different clubs got in touch to express their grief and to describe the huge impact the Great Man had on football and their own lives. Chris Harrison, a Manchester United supporter, summed-up many tributes when he e-mailed to say: "Brian left his mark on all of us…RIP Cloughie and thanks for the memories. We all died a little the day you left us!" Forest fan Anthony Morris was among those who wished Cloughie had become a Sir: "In my eyes he was the best there ever was and will be. I will always be saddened that the Great Man was never recognised for his achievements and given a knighthood. His death will leave a big gap in football."

Throughout the rest of September and into October, I continued to receive e-mails from fans who backed the idea of a posthumous knighthood, an honour bestowed after death. Again, the messages were not just from supporters of clubs he was associated with. A Leicester City fan contacted me to say Cloughie should be given the ultimate accolade. "It is a tragedy that it will now have to be posthumous," he said. "Those responsible for considering the nominations should hang their heads in shame that it was not awarded many years ago." Another e-mail, sent from Jersey, read: "…if there is no knighthood for Brian Clough, following his sad and far too early death, then the honours scheme of our country has turned into a total sham. Knight the hero of our land."

All the messages I received were printed-out and put alongside the petition forms, ready for delivery to Downing Street at the end of October. A few days before Sarah and I made the trip to London, we attended the memorial service at Pride Park in Derby. On a stormy night, with heavy rain and thunder, thousands of fans gathered with Cloughie's family and friends. There were glowing tributes from sporting celebrities. Although the torrential rain left many of us soaked that night, it didn't matter. It was more important to be there and hear the likes of former Forest player Martin O'Neill describe Cloughie as "an incredible manager and an even better man." Brian's wife Barbara read a poem, but before doing so raised a laugh from the stands with a comment about the terrible weather. "It was probably Brian's way of saying, 'I told you I didn't want any fuss.'"

The following week, we met the Derby North MP, Bob Laxton, in London to present the 7,500-name knighthood petition. Sarah had counted all the signatures and e-mails and for several weeks, and many late nights, we had meticulously put the petition forms and e-mails in individual plastic sheets, which were then put inside three large folders. Each folder had a specially-designed front cover featuring the words: "The Ultimate Tribute. Fans call for an honour for Brian Clough." Alongside the text was a picture of Cloughie and photo's of fans presenting the petition forms to me in Middlesbrough, Nottingham, Derby and Burton. Inside, I had written a covering letter to Tony Blair, explaining I had travelled from Nottinghamshire to deliver the petition calling for a posthumous knighthood or similar honour.

The letter to Mr Blair began by describing the background to the campaign and how the calls for an honour for Mr Clough, beyond the OBE already awarded, had increased since his death. The letter continued:

"I am sure you cannot have failed to notice the outpouring of love and admiration following Mr Clough's recent death. He was an exceptional man. Yet long before his death, a campaign had started calling for a knighthood. It united fans from many different clubs and countries, as you will see from the enclosed signatures and messages."

I went on to explain that although a posthumous knighthood had not been given before, I hoped that Mr Blair would respond to public opinion.

"For a man who re-wrote the history books of our national game, the history books should be re-written for him."

The letter, which was on one side of A4 paper, concluded with three sentences:

"Please consider a posthumous knighthood, a similar honour, or perhaps something awarded to his family and widow Barbara, on behalf of fans around the world.

"Thank you for your time in reading this. Please do something to reflect the strong feeling of football supporters in their love and respect for a very special man."

The three folders also included the glowing tribute sent to Nottingham Forest by Sepp Blatter, the President of football's world governing body, FIFA. In a letter written shortly after Cloughie died, Mr Blatter described him as a "gifted mentor and respected manager who brought out the best in players in the clubs he coached." He said Forest's double European Cup success, following straight on from promotion and the league title, "stands out in the history of football as a truly unique achievement."

Armed with the three folders bursting with signatures, e-mails and tributes, Sarah and I met Bob Laxton on October 26th, 2004, at Portcullis House, a modern building opposite the Houses of Parliament. Understandably we had to go through various security checks before being allowed into the building, where many MP's have their offices. Bob was clearly impressed with the work that had gone into preparing the folders. He said petitions handed-in to Number Ten were often just bundles of paper secured with elastic bands. But these looked very professional. We had time for a coffee before the presentation was due to take place and Bob explained the procedure. We were booked-in to handover the petition at Number Ten at 11.30am. The Police would let us through the security cordon but it was vital we were on time. There was also likely to be a media presence there to capture the moment.

As we walked towards Downing Street, I felt proud at what we had achieved so far. I could feel my heart thumping as we were given clearance to go through the security gate and walk onto Downing Street itself. Bob, Sarah and I each held one of the folders as we stood outside Number Ten. This was it. This was what we had worked so hard to make a reality. The many hours collecting signatures and publicising the campaign, the various journeys to collect petition forms, the late-nights spent compiling the folders. But it was all worth it. It was a sunny morning in late October and I couldn't help feeling that Cloughie was giving us his thumbs-up, his approval.

I've often been asked whether Cloughie would have actually accepted the offer of a knighthood - whether he would have been pleased with the recognition from the 'establishment.' In 2001, speaking in a radio interview, the Great Man gave a clear reply: "It would be tremendous," he said. "But I don't decide things like that. I decide where our Queen lives and how much money we give her and mundane things like that. But I don't decide knighthoods."

My hope, that morning in 2004, was that those who do decide such honours would look favourably on our petition. Proudly holding the folders, we paused for a few moments to have photographs taken outside that famous address. The big black door of Number Ten was opened by an official and we handed-over the petition. It was then time to face the media, with various television interviews, including BBC, ITV and Sky. All three of us hoped that the more publicity that was generated, the better chance there might be of the petition succeeding. Bob said although posthumous honours were rare, he would do his best and he hoped all the media coverage would provide sufficient pressure to make it happen.

After the television interviews, Bob took us into the Houses of Parliament where we had a tour and watched one of the parliamentary debates among MP's in the Commons. We also spent a few minutes on the terrace next to the River Thames. And as we sat in the sunshine I felt pleased that at least we had taken the issue right to the very top - just as we had vowed to do. The matter was now out of our hands.

Although we had handed-in the folders at Number Ten, I was keen that Cloughie's family should have the opportunity to see the petition, including the letters and messages of support. So Sarah and I made copies of each sheet, again putting them in plastic covers, and secured them in replica folders. One set was for Mrs Clough, which we gave to her via her son Simon at his shop in Nottingham. It was the first time I had met Simon and I was a little apprehensive because it was a sensitive matter. But I shouldn't have worried. Simon put both myself and Sarah at ease and said how pleased he was to meet us at last. His Mum thanked us personally for passing on all the messages and I know they brought a lot of comfort at a very sad time. We presented the other set of folders to Cloughie's brother and sister, Joe and Doreen, during a memorable trip to Middlesbrough.

That visit was organised for me by a reporter from the Middlesbrough Evening Gazette, whom I had spoken to regularly during the knighthood campaign. Will Sutton arranged for us to meet Joe and Doreen to hand-over the petition folders and, in return, he wrote a report on the visit for the Gazette. It was an honour to meet them and listen to their memories of their brother. I'm very glad to say we've stayed in touch and Sarah and I have visited them again in Middlesbrough several times. On one occasion, after I had the privilege of sitting next to Doreen at Middlesbrough's Riverside Stadium for Colin Cooper's testimonial match, we enjoyed fish and chips back at her home. Doreen recalled many happy memories of Brian. Among the happiest were the days when they lived in Valley Road, where Brian was born. "They were really happy days - when we were all together," said Doreen. "Brian was such a wonderful brother and we always kept in touch. The thing I will always remember is what he would say every time he rang me on the phone. He would ask: 'Is there anything I can get you, because there are only two things I can give. All my love, which you've got, and all my money, which is yours.' That was Brian. And I'll never forget him."

As for Joe - well, he gave me a piece of advice that I will certainly never forget. It was February, 2005, and just a few days after St Valentine's Day. Sarah and I had just enjoyed meeting Joe and Doreen for the first time and were about to say goodbye at the end of our visit. Then Joe asked us if we were 'an item' - were we married? "Well, I guess you'd say we are partners," came the reply. "Partners?" questioned Joe. Then, in a style his brother would have been proud of, he summed-up the necessary course of action in three words: "Get it done."

How could I refuse? With that resounding Clough approval, I popped the question the next day during a visit to Whitby, on the Yorkshire coast. And I'm proud to say the answer was yes. It was therefore fitting that Joe and Doreen were special guests at our wedding in Nottingham. Joe came with his wife June, and Doreen came with her daughter, Debs, and grand-daughter Sally. As you might expect, it was a Clough-themed wedding! (more about that later).

Unfortunately, as far as the knighthood campaign was concerned, it seemed the honours officials had failed to 'get it done.' Within a few days of handing-in the petition, I received a letter from Ten Downing Street, sent on behalf of the Prime Minister. It stated that the PM understood and sympathised with the suggestion of an honour, especially given the pleasure that Cloughie had brought to so many people. "He was a great footballer, coach and manager of the sport and was deservedly awarded the OBE in 1991," said the letter. However, it explained that the Prime Minister was unable to make recommendations to the Queen for posthumous honours, as they are restricted to medals awarded for gallantry only. The letter concluded: "The Prime Minister is sorry to have to send you such a disappointing reply."

That letter was dated October 29th, 2004, just three days after the petition was handed-in. When I told Mike Simpson, he was astounded. "I can't believe they have dismissed such a huge petition so quickly," he said. "The speed with which the reply was written shows they have not looked into the matter seriously. The strong feelings of thousands of fans around the world have been dismissed with one swipe of an official's pen."

A further letter was sent to the Prime Minister, asking for the request for a posthumous honour to be re-considered. Mike said he had been given fresh hope after looking into the case of the golfer Henry Cotton, who was knighted in the 1988 New Year Honours List, after he had died. Mike felt strongly that this set a precedent for bestowing honours posthumously. However, the further reply from Downing Street said Sir Henry's knighthood was not a posthumous award. It explained: "He was 'sounded out' in the normal way and the Queen formally approved the Prime Minister's recommendation. Unfortunately, he died shortly before his award was announced in the New Year Honours List and, of course, before he was able to attend an Investiture to be conferred with the accolade." A further letter from Bob Laxton to Tony Blair drew a similar response.

Undeterred, Sarah then wrote to the Prime Minister and the then Lord Chancellor, Lord Falconer, who lived in Nottinghamshire. She pointed out that if it was not possible to honour Mr Clough posthumously, then perhaps there could be some recognition for his family or specifically for Barbara. In his books, Cloughie said Barbara's love and support was priceless, especially during the difficult times. But again the reply from Downing Street was disappointing. The letter from the Honours Secretary stated: "I have to say that the honours selection committee, which advises the Prime Minister on potential recipients, are unlikely to recommend an honour for any person whose achievement was based on that of the spouse."

Looking back, Mike Simpson said he felt the Labour government should have done more to honour Cloughie. He felt it was ironic that the OBE had been awarded during a Conservative administration. Mike said he was frustrated that Labour, whom Cloughie strongly supported and for whom he had often launched the parliamentary election campaigns of local candidates, didn't return the complement when it mattered. "When

1O DOWNING STREET
LONDON SW1A 2AA

From the Honours Section   29 October 2004

Dear Mr Alton,

The Prime Minister has asked me to thank you for your letter of 26 October, enclosing a petition, recommending a posthumous knighthood for Mr Brian Clough.

The Prime Minister understands and sympathises with your suggestion, especially given the pleasure that he had brought to so many people. He was a great footballer, coach and manager of the sport and was deservedly awarded the OBE in 1991.

I am afraid, however, that the Prime Minister is unable to make recommendations to The Queen for posthumous honours, as there is no provision in the statutes of the various Orders of Chivalry that allows him to do so. Posthumous awards are restricted to medals awarded for gallantry only.

The Prime Minister is sorry to have to send you such a disappointing reply.

Yours sincerely,

Margaret Pickersgill

MARGARET PICKERSGILL

you look at the other figures in football who were knighted, it is astounding that Cloughie was not made a Sir years ago," said Mike. "His achievements far outweigh those of many others, especially when you consider the small resources at his disposal."

Despite the knock-backs and disappointing replies, there is always one thing which I have remained positive about - something which should give a sense of pride to everyone who supported the knighthood petition. It's that Cloughie knew about the campaign before he died - and he could see the real affection and admiration that so many fans felt for him. That's the really important thing. As Alan Curbishley said in his letter to me, "He'll always be a Sir in my eyes." And I'm sure many people share those sentiments - whether they be football fans, or those who didn't follow the game but simply appreciated what Cloughie stood for and felt he was their friend.

And it's that unquestioned admiration from thousands of people around the world which inspired me to embark on another mission - one which I was determined would succeed. My attention switched to creating a lasting tribute to Cloughie, something tangible which everyone could contribute to and be proud of: The People's Statue.

Chapter Seven
We Want A Statue

"We Want A Clough Statue" declared the headline in the local newspaper. The accompanying report summed-up some of the ideas which had been suggested by fans to honour Cloughie. The reporter involved had asked me to comment in my capacity as the editor of the tribute website. I told him that having a statue of the Great Man would be the most fitting lasting tribute. From the e-mails I received, I knew it was a popular proposal. The report said many fans supported the idea. Another suggestion was re-naming the A52 between Nottingham and Derby 'Brian Clough Way.' Although I welcomed the symbolism behind that proposal, and was pleased to see it later come to fruition, I felt that re-naming a dull and dreary dual carriageway after the most colourful manager of all time would only go half the way towards the kind of tribute Cloughie really deserved.

So I set about starting the efforts to have a bronze statue of the Master Manager. Looking back, I probably didn't realise the huge step I was about to take and the many hours that would be spent by a small group of volunteers trying to raise tens of thousands of pounds. But I was determined to get the ball rolling - provided there was the necessary support. I contacted Nottingham Forest and Nottingham City Council to see what they thought of the idea. The initial response from the council leader, Jon Collins, was very encouraging. But it was clear that any fund-raising campaign would have to be led by the fans.

The feedback I received from Forest was that there were no plans for a statue of Cloughie at the City Ground at that stage - it would be dependent on any development of the Main Stand, if that happened sometime in the future. The club had already re-named one if its stands in Cloughie's honour and there was a bust of the Great Man in the reception area. Nevertheless, the club said it was willing to back the idea of a statue in Nottingham and would do all it could to help the campaign. The chairman of the Supporters Club, Paul Ellis, who had helped with the knighthood petition, told me he also liked the idea of having a statue. He agreed with me that if the proposal was to go ahead, it needed to be done as soon as possible and that the impetus for the idea should not be lost.

Having established that a statue was a feasible proposition, I wanted to ensure that Cloughie's family were comfortable with the proposal, before it was taken any further. I wrote to Mrs Clough, explaining that the initial responses I had received were encouraging - and asking whether the idea of a statue in Nottingham city centre would have her support. My letter added that fans in Middlesbrough had already started raising money for a statue there and I was sure that efforts could start in Nottingham very soon if she approved. I was absolutely delighted when Mrs Clough phoned me to say she liked the idea of having a statue in the centre of Nottingham, if the proposal could get off the ground. It was an incredible feeling to receive that phone call and from that moment onwards, I was more determined than ever to make it happen.

Over the next few days I contacted the small group of people who had helped with the knighthood petition in Nottingham. Without hesitation, they were keen to be involved with a statue fund-raising project, whatever form it may take. Sarah had already offered to help me. Her support and passion for the idea was vital. We had agreed, between us, that she should sit on any fund-raising committee that may be set up, while I would provide ideas, advice and other practical help. The fact that Sarah also worked at the city council, and knew who to contact, was crucial in helping to move things forward.

By the end of February 2005, arrangements had been made for a small meeting to be held at Nottingham's Council House. The aim was to see how a statue project could get underway and what backing the city council was prepared to give. Gathered in the Deputy Lord Mayor's Room on February 28th were Paul Ellis, Sarah, Mike Simpson, Rich Fisher (whom I had got to know through the fanzine Blooming Forest) and Stephen Barker from the Chief Executive's office at the city council. I attended in order to take notes. Paul chaired the meeting and it was agreed beyond doubt there was widespread support among the public for the idea of a statue in the city centre. After all, Cloughie's unprecedented success had put Nottingham on the worldwide map and he had been made a Freeman of the City. Therefore, all those around the table that evening agreed that the city centre seemed a highly suitable location, especially as there were no plans for a statue at the City Ground. Even today, Mike Simpson feels it is frustrating to hear some people say that the statue should have been at the ground. "For the record, that idea was clearly a non-starter and without the subsequent fund-raising campaign there would have been no statue at all," says Mike. "Forest's more recent proposals to move from the City Ground have also indicated that the right decision was made."

The meeting agreed that the type of statue and exactly where it may be sited in the city would be decided at a later date. Paul, Sarah, Mike and Rich said they would be prepared to sit on a fund-raising committee and that a public appeal would be made for anyone else who was interested in helping. The volunteers at the meeting were told that the council could offer help by giving the fund its public backing, rather than actively raising money. The impetus would have to come from the fans. There would also be help in the planning and location issues and the commissioning of a statue. The council leader, Jon Collins, joined the meeting in between other engagements and said he would do all he could personally to help the project. He was genuinely enthusiastic and described it as a marvellous idea in tribute to a remarkable man. With such significant support, the mood of the meeting was extremely optimistic.

Rich Fisher recalled: "I went into that meeting not really knowing what to expect. The idea of a statue was great, but could it really happen? By the time the meeting was over, I was sure it could. We knew it would be up to us, as a small group of volunteers, to get the ball rolling. But with the council and Forest behind us, and most importantly the support of Brian Clough's family, it was a challenge we were fully prepared to meet. We couldn't wait to get started."

During that momentus meeting, the title of the committee was agreed: the Brian Clough Statue Fund. It was felt the word 'statue' was important as 'memorial' could suggest any kind of monument. It was also necessary to distinguish it from the Brian Clough Memorial Fund, which had been set-up by his family to distribute donations to worthy causes. The first fund-raising ideas were also discussed at the meeting, ranging from an auction of memorabilia to a football forum involving Nottingham Forest legends. It was suggested that big businesses could also be approached for help. Research indicated that a bronze statue, standing one and half times life-size, could cost about £60,000 - so the fund-raisers would need all the assistance they could get.

A press release was soon sent-out, and widely reported by the media, explaining that fans hoped to set-up a fund for a Brian Clough statue, with the backing of the city council, Forest, the supporters club and Cloughie's family. The release was issued under the banner of 'brianclough.com' and Sarah, as deputy editor of the website, was among those quoted. "A statue of Brian Clough would be a permanent tribute from the people of Nottinghamshire to a man who achieved so much and put the city and county on the map," she said. Although I was not named in the release, we both felt strongly that fans and visitors to Nottingham should have a focal point at which they could pay homage to the man who touched so many lives. It should be a statue easily accessible to everyone at any time of day, and not locked behind gates.

The first meeting of the statue fund committee was held on March 21st, 2005 - it was purely a co-incidence that it fell on what would have been Cloughie's 70th birthday. Again, the meeting was held in the impressive surroundings of the Council House. The council had agreed that the fund's meetings could be held there, provided Sarah was present. Paul Ellis agreed to be the chairman, with the support of other members, and more fund-raising ideas were discussed, including those suggestions e-mailed by fans following the initial reports in the media.

One of the key issues facing the committee was how the fund would be administered - who would look after the money? The council was already looking into how it could act as an 'honest broker' so that people felt confident their donations would be safe. Ideally, the committee wanted the money raised to be held by the council, so it would be publicly accountable. But the authority had not dealt with a public fund like this before, so it was unchartered waters for everyone involved. To help the process, an action plan was drawn-up by the fund to clarify the goals and how they would be achieved. However, one thing was clear - the fund could not start to accept donations before it was agreed who would look after the money.

Several more meetings were held before the volunteers felt confident enough to look at setting an official launch date. There was also the addition of a new committee member, Mick Mellors from the supporters club. Mick had helped to collect signatures for the knighthood petition and was keen to be involved with the statue campaign. The month of June was earmarked for the fund's official launch and plans were drawn-up for a special event to start things in style. Behind the scenes, there was a huge boost when the city council offered to give the fund the huge banners which were made for the civic tribute. The banners, featuring images of Cloughie and some of his famous quotes, had been displayed in the Old Market Square following his death. The committee hoped these rare items would help to raise significant sums of money through auctions and raffles. The city council's offer was warmly welcomed by Paul Ellis. "The banners will always be associated with Nottingham's tribute to Brian Clough and are likely to become collectors' items in the future," said Paul. "To be offered them by the city council was a fantastic gesture."

Another boost came when the actor Colin Tarrant agreed to take part in the launch event. He had the lead role of Cloughie in the tribute play 'Old Big 'Ead in the Spirit of the Man' at Nottingham Playhouse. I had met Colin when the playwright Stephen Lowe invited me along to the playhouse before the production began its highly successful run. Colin is not only a Forest fan but a big admirer of the Great Man and he loved the idea of a statue. The committee knew his presence at the launch would ensure reporters were there to cover it.

But with less than two weeks to go before the launch event, there were huge fears among the committee members that the whole project could fall flat on its face before it had even begun. There was still no final confirmation that the city council had set-up an account for donations. It would be pointless getting the fund underway in a blaze of publicity if there was nowhere for the cash to go. Remembering that Jon Collins had said he would do all he could to help the fund, Paul Ellis sent him an e-mail, asking for his urgent assistance. Following Councillor Collins' intervention, the problem was sorted out within a few days and an account for the fund was set-up at the city council.

An immense amount of planning went into the launch event, which was held on June 17th, 2005. It even involved the tram which was named after the Master Manager. The fund-raisers gathered at the Forest Recreation Ground tram stop, where they met-up with Colin Tarrant for the first set of media interviews. "Brian Clough was a brilliant man, a magical manager and a fantastic character," said Colin. "He transformed this city and put it on the map. I really hope this fund does well and succeeds in achieving a fitting tribute for a national treasure."

Then it arrived - the Brian Clough tram. Sarah had spoken to officials at Nottingham Express Transit who agreed the tram could be used exclusively for the launch event, making it a perfect filming opportunity for the media. By offering various opportunities for filming, photographs and interviews, there was an excellent chance of generating plenty of positive publicity - which would hopefully lead to lots of support and donations. I took photo's for the website as the tram took Colin and members of the committee into the Old Market Square. No detail was over-looked - behind the controls of the tram was a driver who was not only a big Cloughie fan but was also allowed to wear a Forest shirt especially for the journey.

When the tram arrived outside the Council House, the volunteers were met by the council leader, Cllr Collins, who handed-over the 12 big banners which had been displayed in the city centre. Radio and television reporters were there to capture the moment, along with a photographer from the Nottingham Evening Post. The whole event was a massive public relations success.

The fund was soon receiving its first donations - £10 here, £35 there. And they came from all over the country. Within the first few days, one man in London sent a cheque for £100. The money was usually posted to Paul Ellis at his office in the firm of accountants and business advisers, PKF in Nottingham. But the committee knew it was unlikely it could rely on donations alone in order to reach a target of £60,000. "I wasn't really sure how quickly the money would start coming in, or how much we would receive," said Paul. "It was a new experience for all of us but we were determined to come up with the ideas and hard work to make it succeed." Letters were sent to big businesses in Nottingham. The first major cheque came from Experian, who sent £500.

With thousands of pounds still to raise, the committee members pinned their initial hopes on specially-made tribute badges in the shape of Cloughie's famous green sweatshirt. Although the badges would obviously not raise all the money, it would be a good start. The idea had come from fund-raisers collecting money for a statue in Cloughie's hometown, Middlesbrough. They had sold small pin-badges in the shape of a Boro shirt and featuring the words 'Old Big 'Ead.' In Nottingham, the green jumper had become the statue fund's logo, created by graphic designer Alex McKenzie in his spare time. So it made sense to have badges in that shape and colour - and with 'Old Big 'Ead' written in gold across the chest.

The design seemed perfect, but there was still uncertainty among the committee members about how many they might be able to sell. After a lot of deliberation, it was decided to have 3,000 badges made. The bigger the order, the cheaper it was to buy them from the manufacturer. But the next problem was how to pay for them. Fortunately, that was solved by an interest-free loan of £1,500 given generously by the Nottingham Forest Supporters Club.

A few weeks later the badges arrived and were ready to go on sale. To capitalise on publicity, they were launched at the Nottingham Forest Open Day at the City Ground in July 2005. The statue fund had a little stall in the Main Stand Car Park, with a couple of cash tins and several cardboard boxes full of badges. Two of the giant banners donated by the city council served as a backdrop for the stall and posters advertising the badges were put up as well. The response from the public was incredible.

Fans were queuing-up to buy the badges even before the gates had opened. The volunteers had barely opened the first cash tin before the money started rolling in. The badges sold for £2 each, which gave a healthy profit. The publicity in the local media had worked a treat, as fans clamoured to get their hands on these limited edition souvenirs. Paul's eyes lit-up when he saw one of the cash tins bulging with notes and, in true accountant-style, he secured it under his arm and quickly took it away for safe keeping. By the end of a very busy and successful day, around 1,000 badges had been sold. That meant the loan from the supporters club could be repaid, with a substantial profit for the fund too.

The statue fund members continued to sell badges on match days, either in the entrance to the Study Centre at the City Ground or in the supporters club office. On one memorable occasion, later in the campaign, Mike Simpson spotted the MP Kenneth Clarke arriving in the Main Stand car park and was determined to sell him a badge. Fellow volunteer Mick Mellors recalls: "All of a sudden, Mike picked-up a couple of badges, shot out of the door of the Study Centre and raced across the car park like an Olympic sprinter. His mop of grey hair was like a blur as he tried to reach the entrance of the club's reception area before Mr Clarke went inside. It was an amazing sight. But it paid off - Mike ensured we had a famous customer and sold Ken Clarke a badge!"

People could also buy badges by post - and later on-line through the fans' website Lost That Loving Feeling (www.ltlf.co.uk). Orders came from fans all over the world. In Nottingham, the badges were also available at a number of shops, including Simon Clough's newsagents and the City Information Centre next to the Council House. The first 3,000 soon sold out and it was agreed that another batch of 3,000 would be made, while still keeping them as a limited-edition design. Many fans wrote to Paul asking to buy badges and enclosing cheques. Some even added an extra donation to the fund. The badges were posted out and the money was then deposited in the special statue fund account administered by the city council. "The response of fans was absolutely tremendous and went far beyond what we expected," said Paul. "The green sweatshirt design for the badges certainly struck a chord among the supporters and they were proud to wear them in support of the fund and in memory of a great man."

To boost the fund further, the first of the big banners donated by the city council was auctioned on the internet. The double-sided banner, which had been specially-made for the authority and hung outside the city's Council House, featured a picture of Cloughie alongside his famous quote: "If God had wanted us to play football in the clouds, he'd have put grass up there." After a big publicity campaign, in which the auction was launched on the Jo and Twiggy radio show, that unique piece of Cloughie history sold for nearly £1,000. The successful bidder, a pub licensee in Nottinghamshire, was presented with the coveted item pitch-side at the City Ground during the half-time interval at a Forest match.

The fund was well and truly up-and-running and was about to get even stronger. The small group of volunteers felt their efforts were being rewarded and they wanted to build on the initial success. So, having seen the tremendous response to the pin-badges, the committee embarked on another big fund-raising mission based on that famous green sweater.

Chapter Eight
That Green Sweatshirt

A leading football magazine once put Cloughie's green sweatshirt in the top ten of all-time design classics in the beautiful game. It ranked alongside the Adidas Predator football boot and England's 1982 World Cup shirt. I was approached by the journalist concerned, Si Hawkins from Four Four Two, to shed some light on why the Great Man liked to wear the famous top - even changing out of his suit and into the sweater for the 1991 FA Cup Final. Having spoken to Simon Clough about it, I can clear-up any doubts. The green sweatshirt was inspired by Peter Shilton's goalkeeping jersey. When Cloughie saw Shilton wearing the green top with a number one on the back, he said "Hey, I'm the number one around here" and then began wearing them regularly.

The statue fund struck gold when it decided to have some tribute green sweatshirts made especially to sell to fans. Privately, the fund's chairman, Paul Ellis, was not completely convinced they would be successful. But he was persuaded during a committee meeting by Sarah, whose idea it was. She said the jumpers would not only be a great tribute for fans to wear, but would also make ideal presents in the run-up to Christmas. To ensure there was no surplus left unsold, it was agreed that 100 would be made to see how popular they might be.

A Nottingham company called October was chosen to make the sweatshirts, which had an embroidered badge featuring the fund's logo and the words 'Old Big 'Ead.' They were launched before a Forest home match in November, 2005, selling for £20 each. Fans queued-up to buy them and most sizes sold out within two hours before kick-off. It quickly became clear that more would have to be made. Fans who missed-out on the launch day submitted orders in the hope of buying one in the following weeks. The committee decided to have several hundred more sweaters made, ordering them in stages from the manufacturers. Paul and Sarah collected them from the factory and brought them home in huge cardboard boxes. Our living room began to resemble a warehouse as all the jumpers were laid-out on the floor in order to put them in different piles according to their size.

There was a significant endorsement for the sweatshirt idea when one of the customers who came to the supporters club office to buy one was Cloughie's former secretary, Carole Washington. The actor, Colin Tarrant, also donned one of the tribute sweaters to publicise the national tour of the play, 'Old Big 'Ead in the Spirit of the Man.' Needless to say, Sarah felt extremely pleased that her suggestion had proved to be so popular. "I still get a huge sense of pride when I see fans wearing the jumpers at the City Ground," she said. "And the same can be said for the green pin-badges too. They raised such a lot of money and were a classic symbol to show support for the fund and to remember Cloughie's outstanding achievements."

The success of the sweatshirts and the badges helped to take the fund's total to £20,000 by the end of the 2005 - just six months after the launch. But several other big fund-raising initiatives had contributed to that total as well. With the backing of Nottingham Forest, the committee organised a huge match-day collection. A team of twenty volunteers was brought together so that supporters could donate cash before a Reds home game. Looking at the fixtures, the ideal match was the one against Hartlepool, the club where Cloughie started his managerial career. Again, the committee ensured there was plenty of publicity before the day, both in the local press and on the radio, with the event taking the catchy title of 'Collecting for Cloughie.' Rich Fisher had bought some green collection tins (even the colour was appropriate) and there were some larger buckets as well. The volunteers stood at various points outside the City Ground in the hope that fans would donate a pound or two. The response was overwhelming. Some supporters, including Hartlepool fans, were seen dropping fivers into the buckets.

Forest's Chief Executive, Mark Arthur, had kindly agreed that the volunteers who were involved in the collection, including friends of the committee and members of the City Lions, could have complementary tickets to watch the game. So, in a military-style operation just before kick-off, all the collection tins and buckets were given to committee member Paul Lowe for safe keeping. Paul took them home and he and his fiancée spent the night counting all the coins on his living-room floor. There were so many, they didn't finish counting until the early hours.

The collection raised more than £4,000 and the following morning Paul Ellis picked-up the cash in preparation for taking it to the city council the next day. "All the money was put into bags and I got some funny looks from the council staff when I carried it all into the Guildhall foyer," said

Paul. "They'd never seen anything like it!"

Soon after that, the committee auctioned off another of the rare banners. This one featured the Cloughie quote referring to the fact he was overlooked for the England manager's job, despite being the people's choice: "I'm sure the England selectors thought if they took me on and gave me the job, I'd want to run the show. They were shrewd because that's exactly what I would have done." Following a week-long on-line auction, it was sold for nearly £800 to a businessman who wanted to display it in his office.

Another banner was auctioned at a charity dinner for £500 and a few months later the fourth banner was auctioned on the internet for £870. The latter featured a quote which was typical Cloughie. In response to a reporter's question about how he handled players who disagreed with him, he replied: "We talk about it for 20 minutes and then we decide I was right."

Committee member Mick Mellors said he was impressed with how much was raised from the initial auctions for the banners. "To receive more than £3,000 from the sale of the first four banners was superb. And we knew there were more of these rare items to auction, with different quotes on them. It gave everyone involved with the fund a big boost. It was also great to see fans approach us with their own fund-raising ideas too."

One of those fans was my life-long friend Richard Hallam who raised more than £200 by being sponsored to run in the Robin Hood Half Marathon in Nottingham. A fellow runner at the event, Seph Pochin, was also sponsored to raise money for the statue fund. Although they both ran independently, they finished within a few strides of each other. "I was so pleased to make that contribution to the fund," said Richard. "The success that Brian Clough brought to Nottingham was amazing. I wanted to help ensure that his fantastic achievements in putting the city on the world map were properly acknowledged in the form of a statue. It'll be something for future generations to appreciate."

Other fund-raising exploits included the fan who was sponsored to have his long hair completely chopped-off. Cloughie himself would sometimes tell a player to "get your hair cut young man!" So Forest supporter Liam Smyth, who'd had long hair for 15 years, thought it would be fitting to have the long locks lopped for the statue fund. He even received sponsorship pledges from the players and management at Forest.

The venue for the big hair cut was the Southbank Bar, near the City Ground, and it took place before the Reds' home match against Bournemouth in April, 2006. Not only did Liam receive more than £1,000 in sponsorship, but over £300 was raised from a collection and raffle before the hair-raising event.

As well as fans, former players also helped to raise money at various events during the fund's campaign. John McGovern, Kenny Burns and Nigel Jemson agreed to take part in a football forum at Nottingham Forest's Robin Hood Suite. Also on the panel was the journalist John Lawson who worked closely with Cloughie throughout his 18-year reign at the City Ground. The event was organised by the statue fund and Rich Fisher had the task of phoning Nigel Jemson to ask if he would be available to attend.

"I was only about ten when Jemson scored at Wembley against Oldham in the League Cup Final," recalled Rich. "Years later, here I was phoning him to ask if he'd take part in a fund-raising event. I had to pinch myself at times to check it was all really happening." The committee had also got in touch with Trevor Francis after producers at Sky TV passed on a message to him. Francis then phoned Paul Ellis. "I was in the supermarket when he called me on my mobile phone," said Paul. "I couldn't believe I was standing in the aisles between the beans and the biscuits speaking to the man who scored the winning goal in the 1979 European Cup Final. It seemed a bit surreal." Although Francis had a prior engagement which meant he wasn't available for the forum, he wished the fund well and said he hoped it would be a good night. It certainly was.

The evening was hosted by the radio presenter, Mark Dennison, and the fans who attended were able to put their questions to the panel. Asked how he thought Cloughie would feel about supporters raising cash for a statue of him, John Lawson replied: "I think outwardly he would have been embarrassed, but deep down inside he would have been quietly pleased." He also described how he had still met Cloughie following his retirement. "He always said he couldn't have a journalist as a friend," said John, before adding with a twinkle in his eye, "so he said I was nearly a friend!"

Nigel Jemson was full of praise for his former boss. "He was the best manager football has ever had," he said. "He always looked after my family and I will never forget him." John McGovern agreed that Cloughie would always be there to help if any of his players had problems outside football. "He was the greatest. He kept football simple and he looked after his players." Kenny Burns told the forum he used to keep in touch with his old boss. "We lived quite close together. We would talk and he was still as sharp as a tack. He even said to me, 'you were one of those who climbed out of the hotel window after the European Cup Final, weren't you?' I couldn't deny it! I miss him. It's a sadder place without him."

The event, which included a raffle and an auction of memorabilia, raised around £650 for the fund. It also showed the fans, if there was any doubt, the real affection and admiration Cloughie's former players and colleagues felt for him. And, for me, one story still shines out as an example of the Great Man's generosity and caring nature. It goes back to 1979 - four years into John Lawson's working relationship with him. John and his wife Carole had become the proud parents of their only child, Clare. But they were extremely worried after being told that Clare had been born with an eye defect that needed urgent surgery. "Brian got to hear of the problem," said John. "Without hesitation he told me, or should I say ordered me, to find the best eye specialist in the country, get the operation done and send him the bill. I had to convince him that Clare was being operated on by one of the top men in the profession and for weeks he never stopped asking if everything was OK. That was the Brian Clough I knew and it meant so much to me and my family."

Chapter Nine
Celebrity Support

Publicity was key to the whole statue fund project - from the first few weeks of the campaign, to the last few days. Carefully written press releases would be issued in the run-up to special events and auctions, with ready-made quotes to ensure the journalists receiving them had all the information they needed. The tribute website became the official site of the fund, which also had its own e-mail address. Fund-raising events were organised in great detail and a huge amount of work was carried out behind the scenes to secure the support of celebrities and leading figures in football to help maintain the media's attention.

It was a letter to the Arsenal manager, Arsene Wenger, which led to more headlines - and one of the most prestigious items donated to the fund. The committee had written to the Gunners boss in the hope he might be able to give something which could be auctioned off. In one of his last interviews, Cloughie praised Wenger and the way his teams played and said they deserved to beat Forest's record of 42 consecutive unbeaten league games. So there was a great sense of excitement among committee members when Arsenal, who had reached the Champions League Final, sent the fund a signed shirt commemorating their last season playing at Highbury. It had 17 signatures, including those of Thierry Henry, Robert Pires and Jose Antonio Reyes. The limited-edition red-currant shirt also came with a certificate of authenticity. It was certainly a fitting gesture, as Arsenal's original red shirts came from Nottingham Forest many years ago. The fund's newest committee member, Paul Lowe, arranged to have the shirt framed and the impressive item was sold for £400 in an on-line auction.

That Arsenal shirt was one of many pieces of football memorabilia which were sold to raise money for the fund on the auction website, e-Bay. Committee member Rich Fisher became the fund's expert on auctioning the various items. He had an account on the website and ensured that the whole operation ran smoothly for the committee, liaising with buyers and ensuring the money raised went to the fund. Even when items were not suitable for posting, he would make sure that the winning bidders received the goods safely. One such item was a football, which was signed by Leicester City players and came in a delicate presentation case. "I met the winning bidder in a service station car park near the A1 and handed over the package," said Rich. "To anyone who didn't know what we were doing, it must have looked very dodgy!"

There were many other pieces of signed memorabilia which raised money for the fund. Forest legend Stuart Pearce sent a signed Manchester City football when he was manager there. Cloughie's hometown club, Middlesbrough, donated a pennant featuring many signatures, including those of Yakubu and Gareth Southgate. That item was sold in an auction which deliberately coincided with Boro's appearance in the 2006 UEFA Cup Final, to guarantee maximum media coverage. The winning bidder paid £500 and the proceeds were split between the funds in Nottingham and Middlesbrough, where fans were raising money for a statue there. The committee also wrote to former Forest players Roy Keane at Manchester United and Steve Stone, who was at Leeds United. The letter to Keane led to another signed pennant, while Leeds - where Cloughie spent just 44 days as manager - sent a signed shirt which was auctioned off in the run-up to the team's appearance in a play-off final in May 2006.

But not all the letters sent by the committee were successful in drumming-up the kind of support the volunteers needed. In 2005, the fund wrote to the East Midlands Development Agency in the hope they could provide some money. An opinion poll conducted for the government agency had named Cloughie as the most influential person in the region. So the committee anticipated a response which would boost the coffers of a fund aiming to publicly salute the Great Man. The reply from the chairman of EMDA, Dr Bryan Jackson, described Brian Clough's contribution to the sporting and cultural life of Nottingham and Derby as "immeasurable." But the letter said that while the agency had named its business conference suite in Brian Clough's memory, and the organisation sponsored the East Midlands Sports Awards (of which the main award was named in honour of Cloughie), it was not able to give money to particular causes like the statue fund. "We have to ensure that the money we allocate reaches projects which contribute directly to our goals in the field of economic development," said Dr Jackson. "It is extremely difficult to single out individual requests from particular counties or cities." The letter concluded: "Nevertheless, we heartily endorse such a laudable project, and wish the venture every possible success."

The committee also wrote to the former England striker Alan Shearer.

Above: Match of the Day. Marcus and Sarah on their wedding day with special guests Colin Tarrant (left) and Cloughie's brother and sister, Joe and Doreen. Photo courtesy of Doug and Joan Cooper (Reflections Photography).

Below: Getting it done. Marcus greets Joe Clough at the wedding reception. When Joe had originally met Sarah and Marcus and was told they were not married, his advice was simple: "Get it done." Photo courtesy of Doug and Joan Cooper (Reflections Photography).

Above: Getting the point. With fund-raising complete, statue fund members hand over a cheque to the leader of Nottingham City Council, Jon Collins, whose personal backing of the fund was vital. Photo courtesy of Neil C Hoyle Photography.

Below: Statue selection. Mrs Clough with Paul Ellis (left) and Cllr David Trimble who were part of the selection panel to choose a sculptor for the Brian Clough statue. Photo courtesy of Neil C Hoyle Photography.

Above: Making 'Old Big 'Ead.' Sculptor Les Johnson working with part of a wax version of the sculpture, before it went to the foundry to become part of the bronze statue.

Above: Studio visit. Marcus (third from right) with statue fund and council representatives visiting the studio of Les Johnson (second from right) to see the clay sculpture.

Above: Family Pride. Mrs Clough with her sons Simon (left) and Nigel and daughter Eltzabeth after unveiling the bronze statue. Photo courtesy Neil C Hoyle Photography.

Below: A Proud Day. Mrs Clough with statue fund members and Marcus (second right) after the unveiling. Photo courtesy Neil C Hoyle Photography.

Above: Special Moment. Mrs Clough after unveiling Nottingham's bronze statue.
Photo courtesy Neil C Hoyle Photography.

In reply, Paul Ellis received a letter from a sports management firm saying that, due to the overwhelming number of requests for signed memorabilia, they had nothing substantial to donate for auction at that time. A letter was also sent to Sunderland Football Club, where Cloughie's playing career had been cut short due to a knee injury. The reply came from the club's charity, SAFC Foundation. It said that although they recognised the "valuable work" being done, they received thousands of requests for assistance every year and were not able to help the fund at that time. The volunteers also wrote to a charitable trust which they had heard was known for its generosity. They hoped it might lead to a three-figure donation towards such a huge project. There was disappointment when a cheque for £25 arrived in the post.

But the positive replies far outweighed the disappointing ones and the fund continued to receive many items of memorabilia to either auction or raffle off. When the committee wrote to the former England striker Gary Lineker at the BBC, he sent a signed 'Match of the Day' script from the 2005 FA Cup Final coverage. The fund even wrote to Frank Rijkaard, the then manager of Champions League winners Barcelona, and received a signed photo which the committee had framed alongside a team training top. Sam Allardyce sent a shirt signed by himself and his Bolton squad. That was sold for £195. The Nottingham-born fashion designer Sir Paul Smith was also very generous. He donated a number of limited-edition, and brightly-coloured, designer footballs which he had signed personally. The committee decided to auction them off at different stages during the campaign. One sold for £270. Sarah and I took another of the footballs to a charity dinner in Middlesbrough, where Martin O'Neill, John Robertson and Nigel Clough were among the special guests. All three signed the ball and it later fetched more than £100 for the fund in Nottingham. They also signed a tribute green sweatshirt, which the fund had framed and auctioned off for £210, as well as a copy of the commemorative edition of Cloughie's book 'Walking on Water' (£68.50).

As the committee collected more and more items of memorabilia, the idea of auctioning a few at the same time seemed a good one. That led to several 'Grand Internet Auctions' which each ran for ten days. Press releases were sent-out to coincide with the start of these mammoth on-line sales. Again, Rich Fisher was responsible for ensuring all the items appeared on the auction website, with photo's and descriptions. But it was not all plain sailing - or should I say surfing. Internet problems late one night led to fears he might not be able to launch the auction at 6am the next morning, as the media had been told. So he decided to drive round to his brother's house in the early hours and parked outside. Not wanting to wake him up, Rich used a laptop in his car and his brother's wireless connection in order to get the auction ready for the allocated time. "It really was a desperation measure, but I knew Alan wouldn't mind - it was all in a good cause," said Rich. "But before anyone decides to trace Alan's address for free use of his internet, I can assure people it has now been made fully secure!"

One of the biggest items auctioned was a giant photo of Cloughie, signed by Mrs Clough, as well as a number of Nottingham Forest legends and the actor Colin Tarrant. The picture, which is Mrs Clough's favourite public photo of Brian, had been lowered on to the stage of the Nottingham Playhouse at the end of a Gala Performance of the tribute play, 'Old Big 'Ead in the Spirit of the Man,' in May, 2006. Players including John McGovern, John Robertson and Garry Birtles signed the picture that night. The playhouse had staged the Gala Evening to raise money for the statue fund and later presented a cheque for £1,000, which included £450 from the successful sale of the huge photo in an auction.

By that point in the campaign, the fund stood at more than £35,000, over half way towards the target. The coffers had been boosted by the sale of newly-designed pin-badges. The limited edition souvenirs were specially designed to complement the original 'Old Big 'Ead' badges which had completely sold out. The new ones were still in the shape of Cloughie's famous green sweatshirt, but instead of featuring the front of the jersey, they showed the back, with 'Cloughie' written in gold across the top, along with the figure of a big number one below. "I think the simple design said it all," commented Paul Ellis. "In his famous quote, Cloughie himself said he wasn't the best manager in the business, but he was in the top one."

Five-thousand of the new badges were made and once again they were a huge success. Fans queued on match days to buy them, as the fund's volunteers manned a stall in Forest's Study Centre. To ensure the money raised was kept safe during the game, Jim King from the Reds' Academy would diligently lock the cash away and then meet-up with the fund-raisers after the match to unlock the door. The total amount raised from badge sales, including both designs, was around £15,000.

"The badges were a fantastic way of raising a lot of money and for fans to show their support of the fund and love of the Great Man," said Paul. "We certainly hit on the right idea when we had them made. Even now, people still ask if they can buy the original 'Old Big 'Ead' badges, but the fund sold them all. They were a classic design." As the fund's total steadily grew, behind the scenes the committee was busy gearing-up for a special event. It proved to be the highlight of the whole campaign.

Chapter Ten
Smashing The Target

When Mrs Clough and her family agreed to attend the statue fund's Gala Dinner, the volunteers organising the event knew it was going to be a special night. And the setting was impressive too. The city council had offered the fund the free use of the Ballroom in Nottingham's Council House. The grand surroundings had been the scene of many trophy celebrations for Cloughie's teams and it seemed a perfect venue for a big fund-raising dinner.

As the plans for the event were drawn-up, the committee breathed a sigh of relief when the Nottingham Forest chairman, Nigel Doughty, agreed to personally sponsor the dinner. It meant that much of the money raised from selling tickets and holding an auction and raffle on the night would be clear profit. Forest also agreed to have a table of 10 people.

But there was still a massive amount of work to do in preparation for the big night, not least of which was selling all the tickets. There were 20 tables in total and they had to be filled. To make that happen, the fund needed a top-notch guest speaker - a famous name who could attract people from big businesses and organisations as well as individual fans. Paul Lowe told his fellow committee members that he would use his contacts to find the right person. It was a sheer masterstroke when Paul secured the services of the former Cloughie player Duncan McKenzie. With a fantastic reputation for after-dinner speaking, McKenzie was an ideal choice - and someone that fans in Nottingham did not hear from very often, despite him being a former Forest star. He'd started his career with the Reds before Clough signed him at Leeds United.

Using his experience of organising similar events, Paul also said he would arrange to have a few members of Forest's European Cup winning squad at the dinner too. On top of that, he was able to confirm a compere for the evening - the local television presenter Dennis Coath who was then working for the firm, The Media Group. To complete the star-studded line-up, the committee also contacted the Nottingham Playhouse, where officials said the cast of the Cloughie tribute play would make a special appearance after their performance that night, June 7th, 2006. So, as far as celebrity guests were concerned, things were looking really good. But the big challenge for the committee remained selling all the tickets - as well as organising the dinner itself. A press release was issued promoting the event and listing the special guests who were due to attend.

The initial publicity led to several tables being sold straightaway. Each ticket cost £40, which included a canapé reception and four-course meal. Sarah dealt with the caterers, after obtaining various quotes, and made arrangements for a mobile bar. She also kept a spreadsheet of which tables were full and which still needed to be sold, as well ensuring tickets were posted out and wine orders were made in advance. "I was on the phone to the chairman, Paul Ellis, four or five times a day, as we tried to sort everything out," said Sarah. "We'd never arranged anything like this before and it became very stressful at times. We were trying to fit it all round our full-time jobs, so it was a big challenge. The committee's monthly meetings became a lot more frequent as we put the event together. But it all came right in the end and it was well worth all the anxious phone calls and late nights spent at the computer."

Paul Ellis' contacts in the world of business meant that many tables of 10 were sold to big financial companies based in Nottingham. And one businessman went to great lengths to attend the dinner. He got in touch with Paul Ellis to say he was travelling from the Cayman Islands in the Caribbean! It was also vital that tickets were available over the internet and many were sold via the fans' website, Lost That Loving Feeling. Other organisations which bought tables included the Nottinghamshire Football Association and Derbyshire County Council. The city council leader, Jon Collins, whose personal backing had been crucial to the fund, was also at the dinner. The fund's committee members had two tables and everyone paid for their own tickets.

With a number of seats still unsold, another press release went out in a final publicity push. To give the media a different angle, the release focussed on Gary Lineker's signed 'Match of the Day' script which the committee had decided would be part of an auction of memorabilia on the night. In a letter accompanying the special donation, Lineker had written: "Brian Clough was a great manager. I'm more than happy to provide something to be auctioned to raise money for such a good cause. I'm sure Brian would be delighted with the prospect of a statue and I look forward to hearing when it will be unveiled." The press release did the trick. The local media reported Lineker's backing and the extra publicity helped the event to become a sell-out.

The night itself was unforgettable. Everyone was delighted to see Mrs Clough and her family. She was accompanied by her daughter, Elizabeth, and her son Simon and his wife Susan, as well as their son Stephen. Laughter soon filled the Ballroom as Duncan McKenzie told some of the stories from his career. Flamboyant as a player, he was equally entertaining as a guest speaker. In one anecdote he described Cloughie's reaction when he asked the Master Manager for two complementary tickets for his parents for a Charity Shield match at Wembley. Clough replied: "If your mother and father won't pay to see you play, how can you expect anyone else to?" McKenzie went on to describe Brian as "the best manager ever." And he had a simple message for the fund-raisers: "I wish you every success and I know you will reach your target." There were also anecdotes from Forest legends John McGovern, John Robertson and John O'Hare as Dennis Coath interviewed them at their table. Dennis also read-out good luck messages for the event from Gary Lineker, Stuart Pearce and Sam Allardyce.

Then came a part of the evening in which it was my turn to take the microphone and make a special presentation to Mrs Clough. It involved a signed tribute by Sir Terry Wogan, one of Cloughie's favourite radio presenters. The committee had written to him after the Clough family released a statement in March, 2006, saying how much they appreciated the road signs naming the A52 'Brian Clough Way' between Nottingham and Derby. They said Brian would have been amazed but genuinely appreciative. The statement added: "On a lighter note, he often cursed sitting in traffic but said how the brilliant Terry Wogan got him to work in a good mood and ready for anything." When I read those words, I knew it was worth writing to Sir Terry at BBC Radio Two to see if he could send something for the dinner. In response, the statue fund received a personally signed tribute from the television and radio star, describing Cloughie as a remarkable man. The committee then had the tribute framed alongside the statue fund logo.

As I addressed the guests at the dinner and began to explain the background behind the gift, I could see Mrs Clough was genuinely touched by the thought that had gone into obtaining it. I felt immensely proud to make the presentation. She thanked me for the tribute and we posed for photographs. Mrs Clough then praised all the volunteers involved with the statue fund. She told the guests: "It has been a wonderful evening. You have worked so hard and I'd like to thank everyone who has been involved in helping to raise money. I'm sure we'll get there. Thank you all so much."

Mrs Clough handed the microphone back to me and as I began to conclude my speech, I could see the first cast members of the tribute play appear just behind the doors of the Ballroom. Colin Tarrant arrived first, then several others joined him. I continued talking until I could see them all and then introduced them. There was huge applause as Colin led his colleagues into the room before Dennis interviewed them, one by one. It was the icing on the cake. Everything had gone to plan, the guests had enjoyed themselves and the evening had been a massive fund-raising success too.

The auction of memorabilia, conducted brilliantly and with much humour by Duncan McKenzie, raised more than £2,000 alone. The signed Lineker script went for £100. Other items included a book signed by Cloughie himself, which I donated through the tribute website, and a football signed by Nigel Clough and other former Forest stars, which was given to the fund by the Nottingham Playhouse. Artist Neil Heath donated a painting of Reds legend Stuart Pearce. Meanwhile, committee member Mike Simpson had been given the task of asking all the special guests to sign several tribute green sweatshirts. One of those was also auctioned on the night, while the others were kept for future fund-raising events. There was another boost for the coffers when Paul Ellis was presented with a cheque for nearly £3,000 from the Lost That Loving Feeling website, thanks to on-line sales of badges and tickets for the dinner.

Although Nigel Doughty could not make it to the event due to a prior engagement, a representative of Nottingham Forest was presented with a framed Cloughie tribute from the statue fund on his behalf. It was a large colour photo of the Great Man walking out onto the Wembley pitch for the 1991 FA Cup Final. Forest had also given one of the star prizes in the dinner's raffle - two tickets in the club's directors box at a home match. Other prizes included two tickets for the final performance of the Cloughie tribute play, plus a meal for two at Cloughie's Carvery in Ilkeston. And if that wasn't enough to tempt guests to buy a ticket, another prize was a 'Match of the Day' DVD personally signed by John Motson. The committee had written to 'Motty' following his support of the knighthood campaign.

By the end of a spectacular night, around £9,000 had been raised, taking the fund's total to approximately £45,000. "For me, that dinner was certainly the highlight of the whole campaign," said Paul Ellis, as he looked back several years later. "We had all the ingredients for a perfect fund-raising event. I thought it was tremendous to see big businesses and individual fans there. And to have Mrs Clough and her family as our guests made it very special indeed."

It was during the Gala Dinner that Brian's family approached Sarah and I with the offer of a special item for a future auction - a bust of the Great Man. Complete with presentation box, it was one of the first to be made and had 'Number 5' stamped on the bottom. The bust was a miniature of the one which stands in the reception area at Forest. The committee decided to make it the star item in the fund's first 'Grand Internet Auction' which was launched in September, 2006. Lasting for ten days, the on-line auction raised nearly £3,000, with the bust itself fetching £770. Among the other rare items were one of the banners from the civic tribute, an 'Old Big 'Ead' green sweatshirt signed by Forest legends and Barbara Clough (from the Gala Dinner) and an original silver-plated tankard from the 1980 League Cup Final, donated by the former Nottingham Forest secretary, Ken Smales.

One of the more quirky items in that auction was a dart board signed by Jim Bowen, who used to host the popular television programme, Bullseye. For anyone not familiar with the game-show, it was a mixture of a quiz and a darts competition. Rich Fisher had met Jim during a personal appearance at a club in Nottingham and asked him to sign the dart board in the hope it would make some money for the fund. The comedian was only too happy to help. "Brian Clough was a legend," he said as he signed a personal message. Throughout the fund-raising campaign, Rich went the extra mile to meet people who might be able to support the cause. He helped to grab more headlines for the fund after meeting one of the Master Manager's first ever signings. Nottingham-born Mick Somers was bought by Clough in 1965, shortly after he began his first managerial post at Hartlepool United. Rich asked Mick if he would back the statue fund - and he did, leading to a substantial report in the local paper.

Another significant meeting for Rich was with a man who was born in Cloughie's hometown, Middlesbrough, and had since become the owner of Garforth Town FC and had set-up an empire of Brazilian soccer schools. The businessman, a big fan of Brian Clough, had got in touch with the statue fund and offered to help. Rich went to meet him and he not only bought one of the massive Cloughie banners for £2,000 (measuring 24-feet high, the banner had hung on the front of Nottingham's Council House for the civic tribute) but he also donated various items to be auctioned, including a football signed by Brazilian legend Pele.

As the fund started to close-in on its target, the committee launched another money-spinning initiative: Cloughie key-rings. Capitalising on the success of the pin-badges, they were still in the shape of the green sweatshirt and combined the two previous badge designs. The limited edition metal key-rings showed the back of the jumper, with the words 'Old Big 'Ead' and a big number one. They went on sale at Forest's home match against Bristol City in October, 2006, and 400 were sold on that first day. That brought-in more than £1,000, taking the fund's total to around £50,000. The fund continued to sell the key-rings on match days and they were also available at Simon Clough's shop and on-line, with the hope they would make good stocking-fillers for Christmas.

With about £10,000 still to be raised, the volunteers felt they were on the home-straight of a marathon. The previous few months had been highly successful. As well as the dinner, the fund's stall at the Nottingham Forest Open Day had already generated more than £660 and there were further significant contributions from banner auctions. During November, a second 'Grand Internet Auction' raised more than £1,400 and included buyers from Australia and the United States. Among the items was the Pele football, along with memorabilia that Sarah and I had asked Nigel Clough, Martin O'Neill and John Robertson to sign at a charity dinner. One of the more unusual lots was a tree donated by the then High Sheriff of Nottinghamshire, Christopher Battiscombe-Scott.

It seemed the fund was agonisingly close to its target, but still needed another burst of energy to help it towards the finish line. The much-needed inspiration came from music - or more accurately a singer from a Nottingham band. Dave Marmion had contacted the statue fund with the idea of holding a Live Aid-style music event. He was willing to get a number of groups together, including his own band The Fakers, to perform and raise money for the fund. It immediately captured the imagination of Rich Fisher who suggested that the former Forest captain John McGovern would be the ideal host, not only because of his obvious links with Cloughie but because of his love of rock music too. Rich phoned McGovern to ask him. "It seemed strange ringing the double European Cup winning captain to see if he'd host a music event. It must have sounded a really unusual request to him," said Rich. "But he was very enthusiastic and said he would look forward to it."

And so 'Clough Aid' was born. Dave Marmion arranged for the Rescue Rooms in Nottingham to stage the event with no charge and he confirmed all the arrangements with a number of local bands. Dave himself had special memories of Cloughie. He recalled: "Back in the early 1990s when Brian Clough was still manager at Forest, I got to be the mascot at a match. I was eight years old at the time, and as I was running off the pitch, Cloughie stood up and shouted to me, 'Come over here and give your Grandad Clough a hug!' I think that's a good measure of how Forest fans see Brian - with the love of a family member. That's why I wanted to get involved in helping the statue fund - and with me being in a band, putting on a gig seemed to be the obvious thing to do to raise some money."

On the night, Rich helped behind the scenes, alongside his brother Alan. The fund also had a stall selling badges. Moments before the event began, Rich stood at the side of the stage and spoke to John McGovern. "I was about to introduce him to the crowd," said Rich. "Knowing that he did a lot of after-dinner speeches, I said that he must be used to doing this sort of thing and speaking to a large group of people. But he said he felt more comfortable running onto the pitch before 100,000 people at Wembley - he said at least he knew what to do there!"

McGovern did a tremendous job that night. As well as introducing the bands, he read-out a statement from Mrs Clough. I had contacted her to see if she would be willing to send a message - and the result was a highlight of the event. It read:

"I don't know where to begin thanking all the people who have supported the statue fund. We are all so touched that so many have been behind the venture, from the people who have bought the badges and key rings, to the ones who have worked so hard behind the scenes."

The message thanked everyone involved with the fund-raising - including Paul Ellis and the committee, Councillor Jon Collins, Nigel Doughty, Colin Tarrant and former players, as well as myself and Sarah.

"We wish you every success with tonight's Clough Aid concert. What a brilliant idea to showcase the talents of local bands and musicians - Brian would certainly have approved, though probably not attended!! Massive thanks go to Dave Marmion for the initial idea and for organising the evening.

"Brian himself would be absolutely amazed at the idea of a statue. I can hear him saying, 'Blow me - I can't believe it!' I know it would have brought a lump to his throat. All I can say, on behalf of his children, grandchildren and his brothers and sisters is a huge and sincere thank you."

Clough Aid attracted more than 300 people and raised more than £2,000. There was also a cheque presentation of nearly £1,500 from the LTLF website, for the sales of key-rings and badges, plus donations. John McGovern definitely enjoyed the event. He told Rich: "The night was certainly right up my street. It probably won't surprise anyone if I said I couldn't live without football... but I couldn't live without music either!"

It was now mid-December and hopes were high that the magical figure of £60,000 could be reached by Christmas. Three days after Clough Aid, the fund's third and final Grand Internet Auction came to a close, raising a further £900. Most of that total came from the sale of the last banner - one of the larger items of the collection and featuring that top quote: "I wouldn't say I was the best manager in the business, but I was in the top one." Without a doubt, the banners donated by the city council made a significant contribution to the fund, raising around £8,000 in total.

There were a few unusual lots in that final major auction. One of them was a section of the original carpet laid inside the Jubilee Club at the City Ground to mark the double European Cup triumphs. The Mansfield MP, Alan Meale, donated a limited edition plate celebrating the 'Nottinghamshire Miner' - with a design featuring a miner's face said to be based on Cloughie himself. In a separate auction to help the fund, Nottingham Forest sold a desk once used by Cloughie at the City Ground.

Despite the success of the auctions, the fund's total stood at £59,000, slightly short of its target. But with the festive season well and truly in full swing, the volunteers on the committee received the best Christmas present they could have hoped for. Donations of £5,000 each from Nottingham City Council and Nottingham Forest meant the fund was completed in style. In football terms, you could say the ball didn't just roll into the net, it rocketed into the top corner with the force of a Cloughie goal (and there were 267 in 296 games for Middlesbrough and Sunderland, he often liked to remind us!). With the target smashed, the committee members enjoyed a Christmas to remember. On Boxing Day, the council and Forest handed over their cheques pitch-side at the City Ground. The following year, a cheque for more than £70,000 (including interest) was presented by the statue fund to the city council leader, Jon Collins, in order for the authority to commission the statue.

The fund's chairman, Paul Ellis, said it was a tremendous achievement to have exceeded the target in such a short period of time. "It was absolutely fantastic and a testament to the hard work of everyone involved in the campaign," he said. "People have taken the fund to their hearts, just as they did the Great Man himself."

The fund-raising celebrations continued when Sarah and I got married - all the statue fund committee members were invited to our Cloughie-themed wedding. And as we prepared for our own 'Match of the Day,' Mrs Clough and her family were extremely kind to us. We were invited over to Derby to see them and enjoyed a wonderful meal as they wished us both well for our future together.

The wedding ceremony was held in the Ballroom of Nottingham Council House. As with the statue fund's Gala Dinner, that impressive setting was highly fitting, having hosted many celebrations for Cloughie's trophy-winning teams. It was great to enjoy the day with our family and friends, as well as our special guests - Brian Clough's brother and sister, Joe and Doreen, from Middlesbrough; and the actor Colin Tarrant.

I had kept in touch with Colin after the fund's launch, so I was absolutely delighted when he agreed to give one of the readings at the wedding. Not only that, but he recited it Cloughie-style. It was a poem I had written especially for the occasion, with plenty of references to the Master Manager. I called it 'Match of the Day' and here's a taster of the final few lines:

"When the fixture was proposed, the players knew that they'd won,
Because the Great Man's brother had told them, 'hey, it's time you got it done!'
But today there's no winners trophy, no victory shield or cup,
Just the celebration of the winning team - and that famous thumbs-up."

Colin's performance was perfect and there was instant applause from all those gathered in the Ballroom. My friend Tim Wedgwood was also in fine form when he gave the other reading, the poem originally recited by Mrs Clough at the memorial service.

The ideal place for our wedding reception was Cloughie's Carvery in Ilkeston, a restaurant opened in memory of Old Big 'Ead. Pictures and memorabilia about our hero adorned the walls, including hand-written tributes from many of his former players. We decided to give all the tables a Clough-related name. The statue fund committee and their guests sat at 'McGovern.' Directly in front of Sarah and I was the table we called

'Cloughie,' at which sat Joe and Doreen, along with Colin. Joe was with his wife, June, and Doreen was accompanied by her daughter Debs and grand-daughter, Sally. We felt very honoured to have them all as our guests on such a special day. Everyone received a little present - the wedding favours were specially-made pin-badges in the shape of Cloughie's green sweatshirt. Unlike the ones made for the statue fund, these featured a copy of the Great Man's famous hand-written message, 'Be Good.'

My Best Man, Richard Hallam, a friend I've known since junior school, said in his speech that Brian Clough was quoted as saying his wedding day, on April 4th 1959, was the most important day of his entire life. "And echoing the Great Man's sentiments, today - in such fantastic surroundings - will be just as special for Marcus and Sarah," said Richard. It was made even more memorable by the unexpected, glorious weather. The forecasters had predicted rain and thunder for our Big Day - but it turned out to be sunny and very warm. Not a drop of rain in sight - not even a cloud dared to make an appearance. I wondered if someone 'upstairs' had been able to have some influence on the matter...

Chapter Eleven
Old Big 'Ead in Bronze

It was a task not for the faint-hearted. Which sculptor would be prepared to put their reputation on the line and create a large bronze statue of the most charismatic man in football, Brian Clough? Although the intense spotlight of international publicity would be an attraction for some people - that same attention could back-fire spectacularly if the chosen artist did not make a sculpture that people could easily recognise.

The statue fund launched its search for a sculptor two months before smashing its financial target. Anticipating that the selection process could be long and complicated, but feeling confident all the money would be raised, the volunteers appealed for artists to get in touch if they were interested in taking-on the challenge of creating Nottingham's lasting tribute to Cloughie. With the approval of the city council, which was officially responsible for commissioning the statue, a press release was sent out to the local and national media, asking sculptors who were interested to contact the statue fund.

The artists who then got in touch were asked to submit ideas for the type of statue they would make, including the size and pose, as well as a financial estimate of the costs. They were also asked to include pictures of their previous work. In its letter to the sculptors, the fund stressed it was looking for "a life-like statue of Mr Clough during his Forest reign." A total of eighteen submissions were received, including one from France.

"It may sound pretty obvious, but it was vital that the statue actually looked like Brian Clough," reflects the statue fund chairman, Paul Ellis. "We had to make sure we got a sculptor who could do that - and then feel confident ourselves that it could be achieved. The controversy over the statue of Southampton legend Ted Bates emphasised how important it was, after there'd been concern that it didn't look like him. Having worked so hard to raise the money, the next step - finding the right artist - seemed even more of a challenge."

Mrs Clough and her family were consulted throughout the various steps of the selection process and were invited to look through all the initial submissions. Some of the proposals were in the form of drawings, but several sculptors actually submitted specially-created miniatures or a bust, to show exactly what they were capable of. The statue fund arranged for Mrs Clough to see the submissions at the home of Paul Ellis. Mrs Clough and her son Simon spent time with the fund volunteers looking at all the proposals, before taking some of them away to show other members of their family. The eighteen proposals were whittled down to just a few.

Officials at the city council also took an important role in making sure that the initial submissions were suitable, before three sculptors made it to the final stage. Again this was with the approval of Mrs Clough, who could not have been more helpful. In dealing with a public work of art, in a prominent city centre location, it was only natural that the council took the lead in commissioning the sculpture. However, along the way, there were times when the statue fund members became frustrated that the wheels of the selection process appeared to be moving very slowly, if at all. When nothing seemed to have progressed after a number of months, the statue fund wrote to the council to ask what was happening. It took the personal intervention of the council leader, Jon Collins, to ensure that things were put back on track.

A shortlist of three sculptors was drawn-up: Les Johnson from Hampshire, Keith Maddison from Northumberland and John McKenna, based in Ayrshire in Scotland. They were each asked to make a miniature statue, called a maquette, as well as a bust. A selection panel organised by the city council would then make the final decision on which sculptor would be awarded the coveted contract. But before that, the three artists' designs went on display to the public in a week-long exhibition at Nottingham's Council House, as well as being shown on my tribute website.

It was important that the public had the opportunity to have their say on the proposals - after all, it was going to be the 'People's Statue,' paid for by money raised by the statue fund. Fans who visited the exhibition were invited to write their comments on postcards. It wasn't a vote as such, more an opportunity for people to say what they liked and didn't like. Visitors to the website could also send their views by e-mail. The selection panel could then consider these opinions when making its decision.

The idea behind asking the sculptors to make a miniature and a bust was that the maquette would show what type of statue they would be able to make, while the bust would demonstrate whether they could re-create the distinct facial features of the Master Manager. The deadline for the artists to submit their work was extended by the city council into January, 2008.

Les Johnson and Keith Maddison brought their submissions to the Council House for the exhibition. These were then put inside glass cases which people could walk around. John McKenna submitted images which were displayed on a board for the public to view. I remember standing in the foyer of the Council House when Les and Keith carried their submissions into the building, a few days before the exhibition. It was wonderful to be one of the first to see the designs close-up - I felt the whole project was taking a massive step forward.

Les Johnson's miniature statue had Cloughie with his hands clasped above his head in a victorious pose - a gesture he often made towards the fans. Keith Maddison created a maquette with the Great Man stepping forward and pointing, as if giving instructions on the touchline. John McKenna's design saw Old Big 'Ead leaning against the Nottingham Forest logo with one arm in the air, as if saluting the supporters.

Not surprisingly, the exhibition attracted a lot of media attention, including radio, television and newspaper reporters. The statue fund chairman, Paul Ellis, found himself conducting one interview after another. He said displaying the designs was an important stage of the whole selection process. "We are looking for a statue which shows Cloughie as everyone remembers him, as the triumphant manager of Nottingham Forest - complete with his famous sweatshirt and tracksuit bottoms," he said. "The final statue will be an important feature of the city centre for generations to come, so it's essential to get it right."

Councillor Jon Collins described it as an exciting time for the statue plans: "The tremendous success of the fund-raisers has shown it is vital that we now have a fitting tribute to Brian Clough. This is a crucial stage of the selection process and we hope many fans will come to the Council House to see the work of the short-listed artists for themselves." And lots of people did. At the end of the exhibition, the work by Les Johnson appeared to be the most popular, according to the comment cards and e-mails. Although as I mentioned earlier, it was not a vote. Here is a small sample of some of those comments written by fans:

"I think the Les Johnson statue is the only one to capture Brian's charm, warmth and character. The bust is a very good likeness. The bust's expression raised a smile too. Also, the two arms aloft pose is one I remember well, looking towards the dug out from the Trent End. All in all, by far my favourite."

"The bust by Les Johnson is the best representation of the great man in my opinion, as it looks the most realistic. Thanks for your campaign."

"The maquette by Keith Maddison is just how I remember Old Big 'Ead on the touchline and it would be a very fitting tribute to the late great man."

"For me it's definitely the maquette by Les Johnson. The pose takes me back to that League Cup final victory against Luton at Wembley in 1989, when Brian waved to the Forest fans in that way depicted by the statue on his way back to the tunnel. What a fabulous memory that is."

"My favourite is Les Johnson's, I like the victorious pose, and his bust showed by far the best resemblance to the Great Man. Congratulations to you all for reaching another fundamental milestone on the journey!"

Among the many other comments was one from a former player who said he was in the youth ranks under Cloughie for five years. He wrote: "The Johnson bust exactly depicts the man." Cloughie's former secretary, Carole Washington, viewed the designs on my website. "He would have been proud whichever one was chosen," she said.

With all the comment cards and e-mails collected, the next stage was for the three sculptors to present their work to the selection panel, which met at the Council House on January 18th, 2008. I had kept in touch with Mrs Clough and asked her if she would be willing to be part of the panel. I was delighted when she said yes - her views and those of her family were vital in the selection process. On the afternoon the panel met, Mrs Clough was accompanied by her son, Simon, and daughter, Elizabeth. Nigel had viewed the submissions at the exhibition. The city council organised the special meeting, which also included the statue fund chairman, Paul Ellis; Councillor David Trimble (with council responsibility for communities, leisure and culture); the city council's Art and Regeneration Co-ordinator, John Hewitt; and an independent arts expert - Neil Walker, the Visual Arts Officer from the Djanogly Art Gallery at the University of Nottingham's Lakeside Arts Centre.

Each sculptor was given about 45 minutes in front of the panel. I sat at the back of the room to watch the presentations before the momentous decision was made. Each sculptor was invited to talk about themselves and their work, before focussing on their proposal for the Brian Clough statue and answering questions from the panel members. Once all three presentations were made, the panel looked again at the various miniatures and busts which the sculptors had submitted. Then came the decision - and it was unanimous. Les Johnson was the man to be awarded the prestigious contract.

Afterwards, Mrs Clough told me that although it had been a difficult decision, she was delighted that all the panel members had come to the same conclusion. "There is something very instinctive about Les Johnson's work and I feel confident he can produce a first class statue," she said. "I was very impressed by the likeness of the bust he created - it captures so much of Brian's character." Mrs Clough was also very pleased with the pose in which Brian's hands are clasped above his head. "It has a sense of sharing a celebration with the fans," she told me.

Understandably, Les - a Fellow of the Royal British Society of Sculptors - was absolutely delighted to be awarded the commission. Originally from Australia, Les had moved to the UK in the Seventies - just as Cloughie was about to take Nottingham Forest on that unforgettable journey into Europe. "He's an iconic figure and deserves to be commemorated," Les told me.

"It's a real honour to be selected for such an important project and I'm looking forward to creating a statue that everyone can be proud of." Les also explained the pose to me: "It's really one of celebration. He is acknowledging the crowd - saying we have done it together. I feel it's a strong symbol of his links with the city. Nottingham has done a lot for him and he has done a lot for Nottingham."

At the same time as announcing the decision to select Les as the sculptor, the city council also confirmed where the statue would be placed. The authority had promised the statue fund from the beginning of the campaign that it would provide a prominent location in the city centre. The money was raised on that basis. And the council was true to its word. It was now agreed the site would be close to the Old Market Square, where King Street meets Queen Street. Cloughie would be looking down towards the Council House, where huge crowds used to gather to celebrate his teams' victorious home-comings. Mrs Clough described it as a very fitting place for the statue. So did the Nottingham Evening Post. In its comment column, the paper said that, uniquely for a football manager, Clough was known to people who knew nothing about football. Many people who had never been to a match felt that he was their friend. The Post concluded that it would have been a shame if the statue had been confined to a place visited only by the football community.

Before Les began work on the sculpture, it was agreed there would be a slight change to the pose. Mrs Clough had suggested it could be altered slightly to show a little movement, as if Brian was walking towards the fans. Les was happy to make that change to the design. Initially, the plan was for the statue to depict Cloughie in the European glory years, as well as wearing his iconic green jumper. But as work progressed, I became concerned that the younger-looking face of the sculpture didn't match the era in which he wore the green sweater, which was later in the Eighties. I spoke to Mrs Clough about it and she agreed the face of the statue needed to look a little older. Again, Les made the changes without any fuss.

Mrs Clough also offered to visit Les to help with the statue's facial details. This wasn't unusual, as she had assisted another sculptor to get the face exactly right on the statue unveiled in Middlesbrough the previous year. That one depicted a much younger Cloughie during his playing days. This time, Mrs Clough and her daughter Elizabeth travelled to Les' studio to see the clay sculpture and decide whether the face needed any alterations. But Les had done such a tremendous job that they said the whole statue was exactly right and didn't need any further work.

Shortly after that visit, Mrs Clough phoned me to say how pleased she and Elizabeth were. "When I walked into Les' studio and saw the statue there, it took my breath away," she said. "Elizabeth and I just looked at each other and said 'it's perfection.' Les has done a marvellous job and has captured Brian's personality so remarkably well." I felt a mixture of relief and exhilaration. I was so pleased they both thought it was perfect, I was walking on air for the next few days.

The following week, I went to see the clay sculpture for myself. I travelled down to Hampshire with representatives from the statue fund and the council. As I walked into the studio, the sheer presence of that statue dominated the surroundings. It was absolutely stunning. Les had taken great care over every detail. He had even looked at a pair of Brian's original training shoes, so he could copy them - right down to how the laces were tied. Les had also visited the offices of the Nottingham Evening Post to study hundreds of photo's from the archives. I thanked Les for all his efforts in creating such a life-like figure. But there was still plenty of work to do before the statue was ready to stand in Nottingham city centre.

The next stage in the process involved Les working closely with a foundry in London. A rubber mould of the clay figure was made and then a wax version was created. At this point the statue was in sections, before hot metal was poured and the bronze figure began to take shape. The sections were welded together at the foundry and then the final touches were made, with a surface colour being carefully applied. By October, the bronze figure was completed and ready to be transported by lorry to Nottingham. An unveiling date was announced and plans were drawn-up for a special event. It was a day we had only dreamt about. And it proved to be a very memorable one.

Chapter Twelve
The Big Day

There it was - under cover from prying eyes. Standing under a green drape was the nine-feet high bronze statue, ready to be revealed to thousands of people who had gathered in Nottingham's Old Market Square, as well as thousands more who would watch the event on television. I knew that the moment when Mrs Clough unveiled the stunning sculpture would live with me forever. But the sense of anticipation had been almost unbearable in the days and hours leading-up to that moment on Thursday, November 6th, 2008.

Earlier that week, I had watched as the statue was carefully lowered into position by a crane. It was early on a cold, drizzly Sunday morning, but the small group of us who witnessed the installation knew it was a momentous time - Cloughie had come back to Nottingham, to be immortalised in a city where he was still loved, admired and greatly missed. As I looked on, the top part of the sculpture was covered by plastic, to protect it from the straps which were being used to lift it. A marquee was then erected over the statue, to ensure the Great Man was kept well and truly under wraps over the next few days.

On the morning of the unveiling I felt unbelievably nervous. After all, it was the culmination of so much hard work and planning over a number of years. Everything had led to this day and I desperately wanted things to go smoothly. I decided to wear my lucky 'Cloughie No1' badge which I had bought during all the fund-raising. I had worn it the day Forest had won promotion earlier that year. Surely it would do the trick again and ensure the proceedings would be another triumph?

Not surprisingly, the forthcoming unveiling was the top story on the local radio news bulletins and on the front page of the Nottingham Evening Post. In fact, the event was previewed by both local and national media, who had access to a special - and rare - interview by Mrs Clough, who said Brian would have been amazed to have a statue in his honour. "He would never believe it," she said. "He used to say 'I hope I contributed and I hope somebody liked me.' I think a lot of people did."

By 11am, just two hours before the official unveiling, I was at Nottingham Forest's City Ground to join some of the statue fund committee members and special guests. It was marvellous to see many former players as I stood alongside fund chairman Paul Ellis and welcomed the VIP's. Cloughie's sister Doreen had travelled down from Middlesbrough and I was so pleased to see her again. She gave me a big hug and a kiss. I also met Cloughie's brother Bill for the first time. Then, with less than an hour to go before that special moment, we made our way outside, to the area usually designated for the Forest team bus. Only this time it was a specially chartered coach to take us into the city centre. I felt incredibly privileged to be travelling to the unveiling event along with the Clough family, just a couple of seats behind Mrs Clough and her daughter Elizabeth. Cloughie's eldest brother, Joe, was in great spirits and we shared a joke together. Another coach set-off with a host of former players on board. It must have brought back a few memories for them as they left the City Ground by bus, this time in honour of the Master Manager rather than with him.

As our coach turned into King Street I managed to get my first glimpse of the huge crowd which had gathered in the Old Market Square. It was a sheer sea of faces, simply mind-blowing. More than five-thousand people had turned-out to see the Great Man in bronze. It all seemed surreal. I hadn't dared to predict how many people might come to the unveiling. But the massive gathering of fans, as far as the eye could see, was beyond my wildest dreams. In front of the crowd I could see the long, impressive green drape which had been carefully placed over the statue. It had been specially made by city council staff, who had matched the colour with one of our tribute sweatshirts to make sure the unveiling cloth was 'Cloughie green.'

Our coach stopped outside a restaurant called Vienna, where I joined the statue fund members, Clough family and former players as we gathered just half an hour before the unveiling. Everything had been organised with military precision - no detail was overlooked. In the weeks leading up to the big day, the city council and statue fund had been working closely with a company called The Media Group, who had experience of managing big events such as this. They had set-up a huge screen outside which showed archive footage of Cloughie, as well as coverage of the unveiling itself. Part of the film showed a short section of a television interview recorded during his retirement. The fans cheered when they saw their hero's face on the screen. "Some people said our success was all a flash in the pan," he told the interviewer. "Well, if it was a flash in the pan, it lasted twenty-odd years," he said. Then a pause and a knowing smile. "Some flash," he added and the crowd in the square cheered even louder.

On a stage next to the statue stood the compere for the event, the TV presenter Gary Newbon, who had interviewed Old Big 'Ead on many occasions. He said that reporting on those glory years was probably one of the best times in his career. Gary welcomed three former players onto the stage, John McGovern, Archie Gemmill and Kenny Burns. All three received a fantastic response from the crowd - and John gave them a Cloughie 'thumbs-up.'

It was marvellous to see so many players from the past who made a special effort to be at the unveiling. A number of my boyhood heroes were there - Tony Woodcock, Garry Birtles, Viv Anderson, Colin Barratt, Frank Gray and Gary Mills - some of the stars of those historic European Cup matches. Plus there were later generations of Forest players, including Nigel Jemson, Steve Sutton, Franz Carr, Chris Fairclough and Kenny Swain. One of the key members of Cloughie's backroom staff, Liam O'Kane, was there too. The Reds manager, Colin Calderwood, brought his Forest squad as well. For a few minutes I stood chatting to the club's chairman, Nigel Doughty, and chief executive, Mark Arthur. They both congratulated me personally for what had been achieved through the statue fund.

Two players from the European Cup years sent video messages which were played on the big screen. Martin O'Neill and John Robertson were unable to be at the unveiling because they were working away with Aston Villa in the UEFA Cup. But the fact they felt passionately enough to record tributes to be played to the crowd spoke volumes about how much they thought of their former boss. "I am really sorry I can't be there in person," said O'Neill, who described the statue as a wonderful honour which was well deserved. "He was an incredible character and a fantastic manager - the most charismatic manager who ever lived," he said. "To Barbara, the boys and Elizabeth, I am sure you are absolutely delighted. I hope you all have a fantastic day. It is so wonderful that he is being received in this manner - and that remains there forever." John Robertson said he couldn't see Cloughie's achievements ever being repeated in the future. "I am really sorry I can't be there at the unveiling of the statue to pay tribute to the greatest manager in British football," he said. There were more loud cheers from the crowd following those video messages.

The anticipation of the big moment, when the statue would be revealed, grew even stronger. Brian's favourite Frank Sinatra song, 'You Make Me Feel So Young,' was played on the loud-speakers, accompanied on the big screen by archive footage from his outstanding career. Mrs Clough was invited onto the stage with her grand-daughter, Natalie, and we knew that special time was so close. Gary Newbon asked her what Brian would have made of it all. Looking at the crowd, Barbara said: "He would have been surprised, but then again, he wouldn't. The Nottingham supporters took him to their hearts and he had a real bond with them. And that shows today."

Then Gary asked Mrs Clough to unveil the statue. I stood in front of the stage, with the media and some of the special guests. I was full of nervous excitement. This is what it was all about. We were about to see Nottingham's lasting tribute to the Great Man. Paid for by the fans. The People's Statue. The large group of press photographers clamoured to get the best pictures, many simply holding their cameras in the air in the hope of grabbing that perfect image, while the television cameras zoomed-in on that historic event. Barbara carefully untied a section of the green drape and the whole piece of silky-looking material slowly slid to the ground, revealing the bronze masterpiece. There were gasps from the crowd and then spontaneous applause and cheers, as they got their first glimpse of the Master Manager standing in his green sweatshirt and tracksuit bottoms, hands clasped above his head, sharing that celebration with the fans.

I felt a tingle down the spine as I stared at that imposing figure and listened to the tremendous response from the crowd. As Mrs Clough had said previously, the likeness of the statue was absolutely perfect. It caught that twinkle in the eye, that special character. I looked across and saw a beaming smile on Mrs Clough's face and I knew it had all been worthwhile. For a moment I simply stood still, immensely proud, soaking up the atmosphere, taking it all in. I looked at Sarah and we gave each other a knowing smile. We had lived and breathed the statue project for almost four years. There were times it had completely dominated our lives. But to now honour our hero in such a special way, and see the thousands of people join in with the celebration, was something that we will never forget.

There was a mixture of so many different emotions for me. Relief that everything had gone smoothly. Excitement at being closely involved in such a massive and successful event which had meant so much to me.

Pride that Mrs Clough was so pleased with the statue. And sheer delight that a dream had come true. This would be a statue at which people could pay homage to the Master Manager in years to come. And not just football fans, but all visitors to Nottingham - a city which was put on the map by this remarkable man and which, in turn, made him an Honorary Freeman.

"It's absolutely wonderful," Mrs Clough told me later. "We can't thank you enough for all you've done. It's all been absolutely tremendous." Her son Simon said it was very special. "For so many people to still feel so much affection for him and to have him in their hearts means so much," he said. Nigel described it as a lovely tribute. Referring to the sculptor Les Johnson, who had proudly watched the unveiling, he said: "He's done a spectacular job on it. It is easy to capture a likeness, but he has got the character as well."

Les was understandably very pleased with the compliments he received and to be part of such a memorable day. "It was a real privilege to create a statue of someone as well known and loved as Brian Clough," he said. "The secret was to capture that twinkle in the eye. It's an honour to think my work will now stand in Nottingham city centre for years to come, in recognition of a fantastic man who touched so many lives. In working on this statue, he's certainly touched my life in a very special way and I am extremely proud to have been involved in this lasting tribute."

Many of the former players were full of praise too. Viv Anderson said he was very impressed with the statue: "It's a remarkable day for the players and supporters. It's a great tribute to him." Kenny Burns said: "It looks very much like him. But I never saw him as quiet as this! It's a great tribute for him." Nigel Jemson added: "You look at him and it's as if he's still alive, as if he's still here. Everyone connected with this has done a brilliant job."

Tony Woodcock added: "As a Nottingham boy, born and bred, I think it is a fantastic tribute in the city centre." Cloughie's captain John McGovern said: "It is a fantastic tribute and well deserved. They have got the image absolutely right." Garry Birtles described the statue as superb. "It epitomises the man brilliantly," he said. "Everyone who raised the money can be proud of what they have achieved. Brian Clough put the city on the map and the turn-out by the public has been brilliant."

Not only was the statue impressive. So were its surroundings. Three of Cloughie's famous quotes had been engraved in the granite paving around the statue. It was a finishing touch which just couldn't be beaten. The quotes had been voted as his all-time top three in an on-line poll by visitors to my website. They were: "I wouldn't say I was the best manager in the business, but I was in the top one"; "If God had wanted us to play football in the clouds, he'd have put grass up there" and "We talk about it for 20 minutes and decide I was right."

The statue fund chairman, Paul Ellis, who conducted countless media interviews that day, said he was delighted that so many people had come to see the statue be unveiled. "I'll never forget this day," he said. "The people of Nottingham can be proud of what they have achieved. It is a fantastic statue which will be here for many years. The statue fund members have done a superb job - they have created a piece of history." The council leader, Jon Collins, whose personal backing of the project had remained vital right until the very end, said: "This is lasting recognition for a remarkable man who did so much for Nottingham and Nottingham Forest. It's been a fantastic effort by the statue fund volunteers and the council has been pleased to support them." Forest's Chief Executive, Mark Arthur, also congratulated the fund: "Not only does the statue look just like the great man, but the people of Nottingham now have a permanent and prominent reminder of all he gave to our club and city."

As well as being interviewed on the day, Simon Clough issued a statement which meant a huge amount to all the statue fund volunteers. "As a family we cannot say enough about those who came up with the idea in the first place and then set about the task of raising so much money for the statue," he said. "Marcus Alton was the instigator of it all and without his idea and persistence the statue fund might never have got off the ground. His wife Sarah, together with Mick Mellors, Mike Simpson, Rich Fisher, Paul Lowe and the chairman, Paul Ellis, then set about the task with great enthusiasm and it must be very rewarding for them now to see the project through to its conclusion. The council leader, Jon Collins, has also been very supportive but I would like to thank everyone who has contributed in any way to making it all possible."

Simon added: "It's amazing really, but working in Nottingham I do realise on a day-to-day basis how much my dad meant to so many people. I get stopped by them so often in the street it's a wonder I get any work done! I know he wasn't everyone's cup of tea - and goodness knows he used to drive me to distraction at times - but there is still enormous warmth and emotion shown to him 15 years after he left Forest and four years after his death. But I can understand it. I'm not a believer in reincarnation but I still get the feeling that he's going to walk back into my life at some stage. He had that kind of presence that no one forgets."

Back at Nottingham Forest after the unveiling, Paul Ellis presented Mrs Clough with a bouquet of flowers. It had been an incredible day. Spectacular and emotional. Just like the Great Man himself. And there'd been a bonus - the weather had been very kind to us all. Earlier in the week, the forecast had predicted heavy rain for the big day. But once again, against the odds, it had stayed dry - our carefully chosen 'Cloughie green' umbrellas were not needed. I suspect someone with some influence 'upstairs' had cleared away the dark clouds. And, if he was looking down on us, as that green drape revealed a stunning bronze tribute, I hoped I was able to make his day again.